Valuing The New Urbanism

The Impact of the New Urbanism On Prices of Single-Family Homes

Mark J. Eppli and Charles C. Tu

Urban Land Institute

About ULI–the Urban Land Institute

ULI–the Urban Land Institute is a non-profit education and research institute that is supported and directed by its members. Its mission is to provide responsible leadership in the use of land to enhance the total environment.

ULI sponsors educational programs and forums to encourage an open international exchange of ideas and sharing of experience; initiates research that anticipates emerging land use trends and issues and proposes creative solutions based on that research; provides advisory services; and publishes a wide variety of materials to disseminate information on land use and development.

Established in 1936, the Institute today has more than 15,000 members and associates from 50 countries representing the entire spectrum of the land use and development disciplines. They include developers, builders, property owners, investors, architects, public officials, planners, real estate brokers, appraisers, attorneys, engineers, financiers, academics, students, and librarians. ULI members contribute to higher standards of land use by sharing their knowledge and experience. The Institute has long been recognized as one of the country's most respected and widely quoted sources of objective information on urban planning, growth, and development.

Richard M. Rosan
President

Project Staff

Rachelle L. Levitt
Senior Vice President, Policy and Practice
Publisher

Gayle Berens
Vice President, Real Estate Development Practice
Project Director

Nancy H. Stewart
Director, Book Program

Barbara M. Fishel/Editech
Manuscript Editor

Betsy Van Buskirk
Art Director

Jeanne Berger Design
Book Design/Layout

Meg Batdorff
Cover Design

Joanne Nanez
Word Processing Specialist

Diann Stanley-Austin
Associate Director of Publishing Operations

Recommended bibliographic listing:
Eppli, Mark J., and Charles C. Tu. *Valuing the New Urbanism: The Impact of the New Urbanism on Prices of Single-Family Homes.* Washington, D.C.: ULI–the Urban Land Institute, 1999.

ULI Catalog Number: V06
International Standard Book Number: 0-87420-826-2
Library of Congress Catalog Card Number: 99-63904

© 1999 by ULI–the Urban Land Institute
1025 Thomas Jefferson Street, N.W.
Suite 500 West
Washington, D.C. 20007-5201

Second Printing 2000

About the Authors

Mark J. Eppli is an associate professor of finance and real estate in the Finance Department at The George Washington University, where he directs the M.B.A. program in real estate and urban development. He also is an instructor for ULI's Real Estate School. He earned his Ph.D., M.S., and B.B.A. from the University of Wisconsin.

Charles C. Tu is an assistant professor in the Finance Department at The George Washington University. He received his M.B.A. and his Ph.D. in finance from The George Washington University.

About CNU, the Congress for the New Urbanism

The Congress for the New Urbanism is a nonprofit membership organization made up of individuals with diverse interests, ranging from architecture and urban design to real estate development, housing and transportation policy, environmental protection, and community and civic activism. Since its inception in 1993, CNU has added members from 18 countries, many of whom are considered leaders in their respective fields.

CNU members believe that the development and restoration of compact, mixed-used, pedestrian-friendly neighborhoods is the best building block for a livable region. These strategies, they believe, are also key to revitalizing our inner cities and helping to mitigate the effects of suburban sprawl. CNU's work focuses on four specific areas: education about design and development; identification of barriers to regional, local, and neighborhood change; development of models and tools that practitioners and policy makers can use as resources; and construction of working relationships with allied organizations to reform current policy.

Valuing the new urbanism

REVIEW COMMITTEE

Preface

This report evolved from a thesis titled "Neotraditional Planning: More Picket Fence for the Penny?" by Leon Vignes in the Master of Urban Planning Department at The George Washington University. His research found that listing prices for single-family homes in the new urbanist community of Kentlands in Gaithersburg, Maryland, were considerably higher than in the surrounding neighborhoods after accounting for differences in lot size, house size, and other factors. We were intrigued by this pricing anomaly, and, using a data set of prices from 2,500 actual transactions, several dozen property attributes, and advanced statistical methods, we conducted a more complete analysis of Kentlands. Our findings confirmed Vignes's preliminary results, and we found that residents of Kentlands pay approximately $24,000 or 12 percent more for housing than residents of surrounding subdivisions (these findings are forthcoming in the Fall 1999 issue of *Real Estate Economics*). In August 1997, we forwarded a completed version of this research to ULI, whose staff suggested members of the Congress for the New Urbanism might be interested in the findings. We subsequently sent the results to Andres Duany of Duany Plater-Zyberk & Company and Todd Zimmerman of Zimmerman/Volk Associates.

Duany and Zimmerman worked with CNU to raise funds to expand the Kentlands research to other new urbanist communi-ties. The money raised for data, travel, and research costs allowed Charles Tu to conduct the research for his dissertation, with Mark Eppli serving as his adviser. We are greatly indebted to CNU for this funding, without which this research would not have been completed. ULI oversaw administration of the research funds, and with the financial and administrative support of CNU, ULI, and the O.T. Carr Scholarship Fund, the Kentlands research was expanded to include four new urbanist communities located across the United States. This report is based on Tu's dissertation, which was successfully defended in March 1999.

We owe a debt of gratitude to the many individuals whose support was invaluable in completing this report. First, we thank Gayle Berens of ULI for her assistance in turning academic research into a "readable" document. Her insights improved all por-tions of this report. We also thank Shelley Poticha and Robert Davis of CNU, and we are grateful for the input from the ten members of the review committee, who provided insightful comments on a range of issues as well as numerous detailed com-ments that have greatly improved the final report. We thank Luis Mejia of The George Washington University and Eliza Webb of the National Cooperative Bank for their helpful comments on an earlier draft of this report. We also thank Barbara Fishel, Nancy Stewart, Betsy Van Buskirk, and

Jeanne Berger for their editorial and artistic assistance.

Last, we thank those who inspired us over the years. For their patience and wisdom, we thank our parents, Elizabeth and Val Eppli and Laura and Wei-Yang Tu. We also thank James D. Shilling and the late James A. Graaskamp for their intellectual inspiration, although we do not hold them responsible for any errors or omissions. Most important, we thank Madeleine Eppli, Eileen Huang, and Eliza Webb for their constant and enthusiastic support.

Contents

Preface v

Executive summary ix

1. **Introduction** 1

2. **What is the new urbanism?** 5
    An Alternative to Suburban Sprawl 6
    Principles of the New Urbanism 6
    Criticisms of the New Urbanism 12
    Do Consumers Prefer the New Urbanism? 14
    Summing up the New Urbanism 15

3. **Selecting the best new urbanist
    developments for this study** 17
    New Urbanist Developments in the United States. 17
    Choosing Communities for the Study Based on Quantitative Factors 17
    Choosing Communities for the Study Based on Qualitative Factors 22

4. **Descriptions of the selected communities** 25
    Kentlands 25
    Harbor Town 27
    Laguna West 28
    Southern Village 30
    Northwest Landing. 31
    Celebration 32

5.   **Statistical methods of comparing home sale prices** 35

     Estimating Single-Family Home Prices Using Regression Analysis 36

     Important Statistics in Regression Analysis 38

     Types of Economic Relationships 38

6.   **Attributes of single-family housing** 41

     Data Sources 41

     Property Attributes 42

     Unusual Sales Transactions 44

     Single-Family Housing Attributes by Community 45

         Kentlands 46

         Harbor Town 47

         Laguna West 50

         Southern Village 52

         Northwest Landing 54

         Celebration 55

         Combined Data Set 57

7.   **How consumers value the attributes**
       of single-family housing 61

     Interpreting the Regression Results 61

     Kentlands 64

     Harbor Town 65

     Laguna West 67

     Southern Village 67

     Combined Data Set 70

8.   **Conclusion** 73

     Appendix: The hedonic price model 75

     Theoretical Foundations of the Hedonic Price Model 75

     Application to the Housing Market 76

     Empirical Issues in the Specification of the Hedonic Function 76

     References 81

Executive summary

Valuing the New Urbanism reports the findings of a study examining the price differential, if any, that homebuyers are willing to pay for housing in communities developed using the principles of the new urbanism compared with conventional housing units in surrounding developments. New urbanist communities were identified using the definition in *New Urban News:* "New urbanist developments generally include an interconnected network of streets and blocks, a clear neighborhood center, a mix of uses and housing types, a compact form, and pedestrian-oriented design with an emphasis on quality civic spaces."

For this study, two primary screening devices were used to select the best and most complete examples of new urbanist development from several markets for comparison with surrounding developments. The first was necessary to address the needs of the statistical models used to estimate the price differential. To run the regression analyses, at least 150 sales of single-family homes in the new urbanist developments were necessary. The second was necessary to establish a reasonable control group. To test the effect of the new urbanism on single-family home prices, a comparable set of transactions was necessary for conventional housing, not developed using the principles of the new urbanism but maintaining all other characteristics of single-family homes. Based on these screening criteria, six new urbanist

communities were selected for the study. Two of the communities (Celebration in Osceola County, Florida, and Northwest Landing in Du Pont, Washington) were later eliminated because of a lack of comparable sales, leaving four in the statistical analysis: Kentlands (Gaithersburg, Maryland), Harbor Town (Memphis, Tennessee), Laguna West (Elk Grove, California), and Southern Village (Chapel Hill, North Carolina).

Information on sales transactions for each market was provided by secondary sources so that other researchers can replicate the findings. Data on single-family sales were provided by First American Real Estate Solutions (FARES, formerly known as Experian), and additional information about specific property attributes came from tax assessment offices in each market. Information for a total of 5,833 sales transactions for 1994 to 1997 was collected in the four different markets, 664 of the transactions in new urbanist developments and 5,169 in conventional developments surrounding the new urbanist developments.

To estimate the price differential between homes in new urbanist developments and those in surrounding conventional developments, it was necessary to account for all other factors that consumers consider when purchasing a single-family home. To isolate the effect of the new urbanism on single-family home prices, between 18 and 32 attributes—including size of the lot, number of covered or enclosed parking spaces, living area, number of bathrooms, existence of a basement, existence of a fireplace, quality of construction, age and location of the property, and year of the sale—were included (controlled for) in several different regression models. The number of attributes varied based on the availability of data in each market. Additionally, a new urbanist attribute was included in each model to estimate the effect of residing in a new urbanist community on the price of single-family sales. In all the analyses, the price of single-family homes was explained using multiple regression analysis, with one of the explanatory variables (i.e., one of the attributes that explain the purchase price of a single-family home) a new urbanism variable.

For each of the four communities and for the combined communities, linear (constant returns-to-scale) and semi-log (diminishing-returns-to-scale) regression results found that across all models (both linear and semi-log) and across all communities, the regression models explained 85 to 92 percent of single-family home sale prices (R-squared). Moreover, the new urbanist attribute (parameter estimate) maintained a positive sign and a t-statistic that is significant at the 99 percent level. In other words, homeowners paid more to live in new urbanist developments compared with the areas surrounding new urbanist communities. This price differential controlled for differentials in lot size, number of covered or enclosed parking stalls, living area, number of bathrooms, existence of a basement, number of fireplaces, construction quality, age and location of the property, and year of sale, among other factors. Simply stated, consumers pay more for the same home in a new urbanist development.

The estimated price differential between single-family homes in new urbanist developments and in the areas surrounding them varied among the four developments studied. This price differential was statistically significant and of a sizable magnitude in all cases, ranging from $5,000 to $30,000 for the individual developments and $20,000 for the combined developments. Although no model can perfectly separate the effects of the new urbanism from other housing characteristics, the size and consistency of the premium for the new urbanism suggest that consumers are willing to pay more to reside in such communities.

Estimated New Urbanism Premium

	Dollar Value	Percent of Home Value
Kentlands	$ 24,603	13
Harbor Town	30,690	25
Laguna West	5,157	4
Southern Village	16,334	9
Combined	20,189	11

Based on these findings, it is clear that consumers paid more to live in new urbanist communities, although the interpretation of this premium involves some limitations. The premium is relative to the price of single-family homes in the areas surrounding new urbanist developments for 1994 to 1997 and does not indicate that developers make more money developing new urbanist communities. Similarly, it is impossible at this point to determine whether the premium reflects the behavior of all or even a majority of homebuyers. Although this report presents some new findings on consumers' preferences in choosing where to reside, future research is necessary on this important issue.

1

Introduction

The new urbanism has been a prevalent topic in planning and real estate development over the past few years. Newsweek *and* Consumer Reports *have published special reports that describe the characteristics of the new urbanism,[1]* ABC News Nightline *aired a show introducing the new urbanism to the television-viewing public, and numerous articles about the new urbanism have appeared in the nation's leading newspapers.[2] While the new urbanism has been popular in the press, the benefits and desirability for consumers of new urbanist development are being intensely debated in planning and municipal offices and in the halls of academe.[3] Even Hollywood's* The Truman Show, *which was filmed at Seaside, arguably the most famous new urbanist community, has initiated some discussion about the communities designed by the new urbanists.[4]*

Proponents of the new urbanism believe that denser, more compact forms of development are a cure for suburban sprawl. Critics, on the other hand, argue that the new urbanism is too concerned with regulating appearance and architectural details and has ignored the more essential social and economic issues in the resulting developments. Other critics claim that consumers simply do not care about the features offered by the new urbanism and that conventional suburban developments provide what homebuyers desire.

Since World War II, suburbia has become most Americans' preferred place to live.[5] The ubiquity of automobiles and advances in the highway transportation

system have provided suburbanites with an opportunity to move away from the challenges of the city. Suburban living is perceived as having many advantages—cleaner air, more green space, greater privacy, and less crime—but the rapid growth in suburban areas has been accompanied by numerous new issues and concerns.

Post–World War II development comes with its problems, particularly suburban sprawl. Suburban development is said to create countless undifferentiated new subdivisions with no sense of place or community. Greenfields and farmland are transformed into houses, shopping centers, and parking lots that consume valuable natural resources. Local governments allocate limited budgets to create new infrastructure, placing less importance on existing services. And isolated land uses cause heavy reliance on automobiles, creating traffic congestion and air pollution.

The new urbanism is one attempt to reform the sprawling pattern of suburban growth. Through a comprehensive strategy of architectural planning and design, the new urbanists attempt to re-create community settings commonly seen in places like Charleston, South Carolina, and Old Town Alexandria, Virginia. These settings provide both inspiration and practical lessons for the design of new communities.[6] Following these traditional examples, the new urbanists favor a concept of residential development that includes small lots, short housing setbacks, alleys, front porches, compact, walkable neighborhoods with abundant public space, a mix of land uses and activities near each other and narrow, interconnected streets.

To date, much of the analysis of the new urbanism has focused on descriptive comparisons between new urbanist and conventional suburban developments. The new urbanism has also been evaluated based on its ability to improve the current development pattern or to solve the problems caused by suburban sprawl. Only a few studies evaluate new urbanist developments from homeowners' point of view. And none of the research addresses the price differentials, if any, between new urbanist and conventional developments.

This report examines the new urbanism from the perspective of the housing market. By comparing the actual sale prices of single-family homes in new urbanist and other developments, it is possible to estimate the price differential between the two development types. In this context, housing is considered as a bundle of housing attributes, including site, structure, neighborhood, and locational characteristics. While consumers do not individually price these attributes,

each attribute influences consumers' decisions about purchasing a home. Then, using the actual property price and the composition of housing traits, it is possible to estimate prices of individual attributes using statistical models. Based on actual records of house transactions, the impact of the new urbanism on prices of single-family homes can be isolated and the question addressed, Are consumers willing to pay more for properties in a new urbanist community than for comparable units in a conventional suburban development?

The rest of this report addresses this question:

- Chapter 2 presents the goals and principles of the new urbanism and reviews the criticisms and market acceptance of new urbanist developments.
- Chapter 3 lays out the criteria for choosing the new urbanist communities for this study, including both quantitative and qualitative factors used to identify the communities that most completely reflect the characteristics of the new urbanism.
- Chapter 4 describes the selected communities.
- Chapter 5 discusses the statistical methods used to isolate the impact of the new urbanism on the prices of single-family homes and explains the important ratios that are commonly used to assess the credibility of a statistical model.
- Chapter 6 presents a comparative discussion of the housing attributes in the selected new urbanist developments and the surrounding areas.
- Chapter 7 explains how consumers value single-family housing.
- Chapter 8 summarizes the report and suggests areas for future inquiry.
- The appendix explains the price model used in the study.

Notes

1. See Adler (1995) and *Consumer Reports* (1996), respectively.

2. For example, *The New York Times* (Boxer 1998; Singer 1998), *The Wall Street Journal* (Binkley 1996; Carrns 1997), *The Washington Post* (Gelfeld 1998; Shields 1998), *Chicago Tribune* (Sherlock 1998), *The Atlanta Journal and Constitution* (McCosh and Soto 1998), *The Boston Globe* (Flint 1998), and *Los Angeles Times* (Damer 1998).

3. See Krieger (1998), Gordon and Richardson (1997), and Ewing (1997) for examples.

4. See Wilson (1998), Kroloff (1998), and Goldberger (1998).

5. According to the *1995 American Housing Survey* (U.S. Bureau of the Census 1995), 58 percent of the households in metropolitan statistical areas are located in suburbs rather than in central cities. The *1997 National Housing Survey* conducted by Fannie Mae (1997) reveals that more than 60 percent of Americans believe overcrowding, congestion, crime, violence, gangs, and racial tensions have increased more in cities than in suburbs.

6. T. Bressi, "Planning the American Dream," in *The New Urbanism: Toward an Architecture of Community,* ed. Peter Katz (New York: McGraw-Hill, 1994), p. xxv.

What is the new urbanism?

CHAPTER 2

The new urbanism has been defined several ways. William Fulton, in The New Urbanism: Hope or Hype for American Communities? *defines it as "a movement in architecture, planning, and urban design that emphasizes a particular set of design principles, including pedestrian- and transit-oriented neighborhood design and a mix of land uses, as a means of creating more cohesive communities."[1] The Congress for the New Urbanism (CNU), which has dominated the research and promotion of the principles of the new urbanism, defines it as a planning approach "that seeks to reintegrate the components of modern life—housing, workplace, shopping, and recreation—into compact pedestrian-friendly mixed-use neighborhoods linked by transit and set in a larger regional open space framework."[2]*

In general, the new urbanists have established a set of design and planning principles meant to restore community life. The principles lay out a broad vision that focuses on integrating all aspects of daily life, from housing and employment to recreation and education, while reducing the use of limited natural resources. By offering diverse styles of housing with a mix of land uses, new urbanist developments attempt to integrate residents' daily activities within walking distance. Through the use of parks, village greens, and other community space, residents have places to interact with the hope of creating a sense of community.

Followers of this movement come from diverse backgrounds, and they have used many different names to describe the new urbanism, calling it, for instance, neotraditional planning, neotraditional development, traditional neighborhood development, transit-oriented development, and the compact city.[3] In 1993, pioneers of the movement formed CNU to promote their ideas and advocate the restructuring of development practices and public policy.[4]

Over the past few years, interest in the new urbanism has grown tremendously, and the number of new urbanist developments planned or under construction in the United States almost doubled from 1996 to 1998 (see Figure 2-1). As of September 1998, new urbanist developments could be found in 35 states (Figure 2-2 shows the distribution of such projects). As the new urbanism gains popularity, understanding its goal and principles, its criticisms, and market acceptance becomes more important.

Figure 2-1
New Urbanist Developments in the United States, 1996–1998

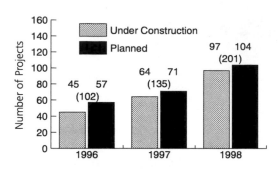

Source: New Urban News, September/October 1998.

Figure 2-2
Distribution of New Urbanist Developments across the United States

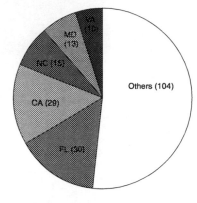

Source: New Urban News, September/October 1998.

An Alternative to Suburban Sprawl

Two primary goals of the new urbanism are to reform the sprawling pattern of development and to provide a form of alternative housing for consumers.[5] As stated in "Charter of the New Urbanism," the new urbanists stand for "the reconfiguration of sprawling suburbs into communities of real neighborhoods and diverse districts . . . ."[6] To understand the principles of the new urbanism, it is necessary to understand the problems caused by suburban sprawl.

Sprawl is generally thought of as a form of low-density development that consists of single-use pods that are predominantly reached by motor vehicles.[7] This development pattern emphasizes expansion of metropolitan areas by converting greenfields and farmland into residential areas and the use of the automobile to increase mobility. A long list of research holds sprawl responsible for many problems: increased vehicle miles traveled, rising infrastructure and public service costs, loss of agricultural and other resource lands, declining environmental quality, and loss of community values.[8] A study of the causes of sprawl in California discusses the costs of sprawl to suburban

taxpayers, farmers, businesses, and the environment, and concludes that the consequences of sprawl affect everyone, regardless of his or her geographical, racial, income, and political status.[9]

Based on a review of the literature on the characteristics, causes, and costs of sprawl, one recommended cure for the sprawling development pattern is "active planning of the type practiced almost everywhere except the United States (and beginning to appear here out of necessity)."[10] Moreover, planning initiatives must be supplemented by government policy.[11] Such a public/private partnership could reform the current pattern of growth and solve, or at least mitigate, the problems of sprawl.

Principles of the New Urbanism

At the center of the new urbanism is a set of design standards often referred to as "neotraditional planning principles." Communities that are designed, planned, and developed in accordance with these guidelines using principles of the new urbanism share the following common characteristics: 1) mixed land uses, 2) mixed housing types, 3) plenty of public space, 4) pedestrian-oriented design, and 5) an interconnected street network.[12]

The new urbanism promotes the idea of balanced land uses to make it easy for residents to walk to work, retail outlets, and commercial services (see Figure 2-3). In new urbanist communities, for instance, a convenience store is considered an appropriate use on a residential street corner, and small offices are permitted in residential areas. Most new developments designed with the

principles of the new urbanism include both residential and commercial components.

New urbanist communities not only blend residential development with retail, office, and industrial uses, but also include a variety of housing types, among them detached houses, townhouses, condominiums, and apartments. The new urbanists suggest that the optimal size for a neighborhood is a quarter-mile radius from the center.[13] Such a compact size and mixed

Figure 2-3

Land Use Patterns: New Urbanist Neighborhood versus Conventional Suburb

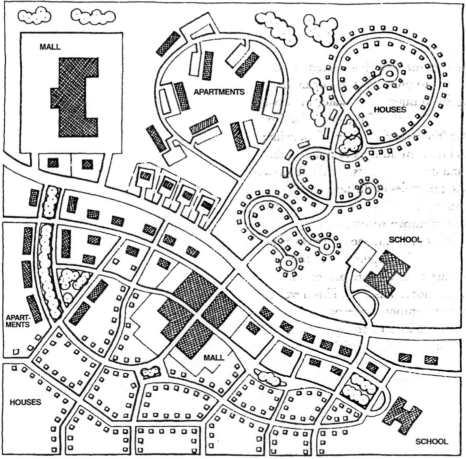

Source: Used with permission from Duany Plater-Zyberk & Company.

land uses place residents' daily living activities within walking distance of home. To shorten the distance from the neighborhood center to its edge while maintaining a number of housing units comparable to conventional subdivisions, the new urbanists reduce the size of residential lots and include townhouses and multi-family units in the development plan, consequently making the density higher. By placing houses close to one another and to the street, and providing more public space, the new urbanists create more opportunities for residents to inter-

act in an attempt to reproduce the sense of community that existed before the post–World War II building boom.

The new urbanism emphasizes the importance of public space that is not unde-velopable residual land. Public space may be in the form of civic buildings or open space. The new urbanists suggest that public buildings, such as town centers, churches, and libraries, should be placed in prominent community locations (see Figure 2-4). Open spaces, such as village squares, parks, and greenbelts, should be provided throughout a neighborhood (see Figure 2-5).

Figure 2-4
Locations of Civic Buildings in a New Urbanist Neighborhood

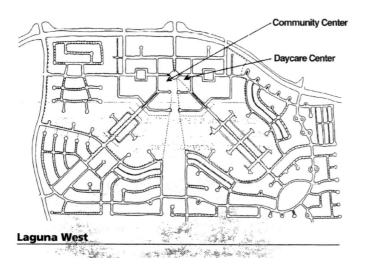

Laguna West

New urbanists suggest that civic build-ings be placed in prominent locations. In Laguna West, for example, the commu-nity center and daycare facility are placed at the intersection of major boulevards where bus service is provided. *Source:* M. Southworth, "Walkable Suburbs? An Evaluation of Neotraditional Communi-ties at the Urban Edge," *Journal of the American Planning Association,* vol. 63, no. 1 (1997), pp. 28–44.

Laguna West Community Center

Figure 2-5
Public Open Space in a New Urbanist Neighborhood

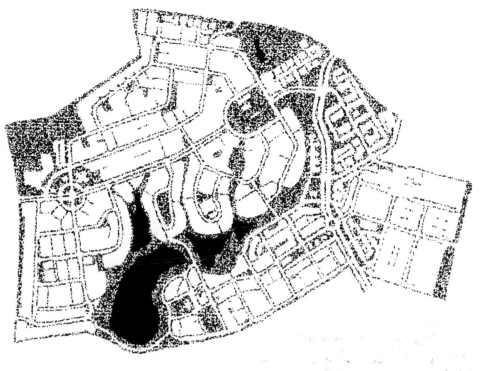

Kentlands

New urbanists suggest that public open spaces be provided in convenient locations throughout the community. Shaded areas represent public open spaces in Kentlands. *Source:* M. Southworth, "Walkable Suburbs? An Evaluation of Neotraditional Communities at the Urban Edge," *Journal of the American Planning Association,* vol. 63, no. 1 (1997), pp. 28–44.

A neighborhood park in Harbor Town

One of the principles of the new urbanism is to get people out of their cars by providing a walkable environment. To encourage pedestrian activity, the new urbanists reduce the width of streets to force cars to slow down and to keep through traffic away from the neighborhood, and use street trees (trees between the street and the sidewalk) and parallel parking to give pedestrians a sense of protection from passing cars. The new urbanists also place houses close to the curb to create the perception of narrower, friendlier streets.

In Harbor Town, streets are narrower and houses closer to the curb to create pedestrian-friendly streets.

In this conventional suburban development in California, streets are wide and houses have deep setbacks.

Another way to improve a community's walkability is to improve the aesthetic beauty of the walk. The streetscape in most conventional suburban developments is dominated by a view of driveways and garage doors. The new urbanists place garages in the rear of the lot and may use alleys to reach garages. In terms of street patterns, the new urbanists replace culs-de-sac, the primary street pattern in conventional suburban developments, with an interconnected street grid. The layout offers pedestrians and drivers alternate routes to their destinations and shortens the distance between two points. Such a street network is expected to diffuse traffic congestion.

Public transit is an important component in new urbanist developments. The higher density of a new urbanist development gathers the population around the neighborhood center, where a transit station is often located, making public transit a viable alternative to driving. Walkability and public transit can reduce residents' reliance on the automobile and make those who do not drive more independent.

The sidewalk in Harbor Town uses street trees placed between the street and the sidewalk and parallel parking to provide pedestrians a sense of protection from passing cars. In a conventional development, trees are placed between the house and the sidewalk.

Criticisms of the New Urbanism

Although architects, planners, environmentalists, and government officials have praised new urbanist solutions to suburban sprawl, this movement is not without its critics. Some researchers suggest that the new urbanists attempt to change human behavior through design, arguing that a planned community using a set of formal guidelines belies the nature of a community.[14] Others claim that instead of mitigating congestion, the neotraditional principles may create more traffic. "Shorter origin-destination distances reduce the average cost per trip," but "cheaper trips mean more vehicle trips, and . . . total vehicle miles traveled may increase."[15] Additionally, many new urbanist developments lack the desirable mix of land uses that create a community, as developers struggle to construct a viable mix of retail, business, civic, and residential buildings.[16]

The streetscape in Southern Village features narrow setbacks with garages in the rear, while the streetscape in a conventional development is punctuated by garage doors.

Another frequent criticism is that the new urbanism creates only upscale projects in the suburbs in green areas (greenfield development). This statement might be true, given the current examples of new urbanist developments, but it is a misperception of what the new urbanism ultimately tries to accomplish. A recent survey notes that "quite a few new [traditional neighborhood developments] are selling and leasing residential units at very affordable prices, and many new projects are breaking ground on inner-city sites."[17]

Some critics question whether the new urbanism provides a desirable alternative to conventional suburban development. In a recent interview, Peter Gordon argued against the new urbanists' claim that in the current market, consumers are not given enough housing choices.[18] He believes that conventional development is driven by the market and that competition will force developers to build whatever consumers desire. "People are getting the neighborhoods they want," he says.

In an address to a group of the new urbanists and academicians, Alex Krieger points out shortcomings of the new urbanism.[19] Although the new urbanists' broad goals of limiting sprawl, minimizing economic segregation, and avoiding environmental deterioration are laudable, to date, the new urbanists have also helped to produce:

> . . . more subdivisions (albeit innovative ones) than towns; . . . densities too low to support much mixed use, much less to support public transportation; relatively homogenous demographic enclaves, not rainbow coalitions; a new, attractive, and desirable form of planned unit development, not yet substantial infill, or even better, connections between new and existing development; . . . a new wave of form-follows-function determinism (oddly modern for such ardent critics of Modernism), implying that community can be assured through design . . . .[20]

The new urbanism will eventually be evaluated on the basis of its achievements, not on its stated claims. As this movement is still in its infancy, whether new urbanist principles can solve the problems associated with sprawl or whether the new urbanism will become the mainstream of residential development remains to be seen.[21]

Do Consumers Prefer the New Urbanism?

Economists, planners, traffic engineers, and even journalists have argued about whether the new urbanism reduces traffic congestion, slows the pace of land consumption, or restores the sense of community. A more pressing question is whether consumers are interested in the amenities offered by the new urbanists. The new urbanism can succeed only if the market accepts the product.

Market Perspectives, a real estate market research firm, surveyed 619 homeowners in four new urbanist communities (Kentlands, Maryland, Harbor Town, Tennessee, Seaside, Florida, and Laguna West, California) to assess the desirability of new urbanist features. Residents in those communities indicated a strong sense of neighborliness, did not think the new urbanism is overrated, were more likely to walk, and believed their homes will appreciate faster than those in conventional subdivisions. Their main complaints were the lack of retail outlets and the slow pace of construction.

Community Planning & Research conducted a different survey during the Vesta Home Show in Memphis in 1993; approximately 600 people responded to this questionnaire.[22] Different from the respondents to the Market Perspectives survey, visitors to the Vesta Home Show were a more representative sample of typical homebuyers. The results indicate that the most desired new urbanist features include small parks and public squares, front porches, and the exterior housing design. Most people do not like the smaller lots. Contradicting some critics' claim that consumers do not care about the characteristics of the new urbanism, two-thirds of the potential homebuyers said they would consider living in a new urbanist development.

An examination of the market success of five early new urbanist projects (Seaside, Kentlands, Harbor Town, Laguna West, and Northwest Landing, Washington) found that, despite the positive results of market surveys, most new urbanist communities have fallen short of original expectations, with the new urbanism's slow market acceptance the result of a lack of market research to determine the most appropriate lot sizes, product mix, and price level; the slow introduction of key amenities; and high density.[23] The study also suggests that more affordably priced housing units should be included in future developments to attract homebuyers.

Southern Village

New urbanists place garage entrances to the rear and use alleys to access garages.

Belmont Forest

Summing up the New Urbanism

The new urbanists' planning philosophy can be summed up in a single word—connection:

First, they try to connect the streets into a network so that people can readily reach other sections of their neighborhood or town. Second, they try to connect residents to shops and services by encouraging retail and institutional development within walking distance of where people live. Third, they try to connect individuals to one another by insisting that walkways be sociable—usually running alongside narrow streets, rows of trees, picket fences, and front porches, balconies, terraces, or other inviting exterior elements of houses. Fourth, they try to bridge the divide of age, household size, and economic status by mixing together houses and apartments of assorted sizes and prices. Fifth, they try to connect the new developments to mass transit. Sixth, they try to connect individuals to civic ideals and public responsibilities.[24]

Notes

1. W. Fulton, *The New Urbanism: Hope or Hype for American Communities?* (Cambridge, Mass.: Lincoln Institute of Land Policy, 1996), p. 2.

2. Congress for the New Urbanism, "Charter of the New Urbanism," CNU IV, May 3–5, 1996, Charleston, South Carolina.

3. See Kunstler (1996, p. 55) and Gordon and Richardson (1997).

4. For more information about CNU, check the organization's website at *http://www.cnu.org.*

5. For more information on problems associated with suburban sprawl and references to additional sources, check the website of *Planning Commissioners Journal* at *http://www.plannersweb.com.* For opposing opinions about suburban sprawl, see Gordon and Richardson (1997) and Henderson and Moore (1998).

6. CNU, "Charter of the New Urbanism."

7. Policy analyst Anthony Downs identified ten "traits" associated with sprawl: 1) unlimited outward extension; 2) low-density residential and commercial settlements; 3) leapfrog development; 4) fragmentation of powers over land use among many small localities; 5) dominance of transportation by private automotive vehicles; 6) no centralized planning or control of land uses; 7) widespread strip commercial development; 8) great fiscal disparities among localities; 9) segregation of types of land uses in different zones; and 10) reliance mainly on the trickle-down or filtering process to provide housing to low-income households (see Downs 1998).

8. P. Miller and J. Moffet, *The Price of Mobility: Uncovering the Hidden Costs of Transportation* (New York: Natural Resources Defense Council, 1993).

9. Bank of America et al., *Beyond Sprawl: New Patterns of Growth to Fit the New California* (San Francisco: Bank of America, 1995).

10. R. Ewing, "Is Los Angeles–Style Sprawl Desirable?" *Journal of the American Planning Association,* vol. 63, no. 1 (1997), p. 118.

11. Ibid.

12. See Bookout (1992a), Adler (1995), and Southworth (1997).

13. See Calthorpe (1989, p. 11) and Duany and Plater-Zyberk (1994, p. xvii). This distance is equivalent to a five-minute walk at an easy pace.

14. See H. Landecker, "Is New Urbanism Good for America?" *Architecture,* April 1996, pp. 68–77.

15. P. Gordon and H.W. Richardson, "Are Compact Cities a Desirable Planning Goal?" *Journal of the American Planning Association,* vol. 63, no. 1 (1997), p. 98.

16. Landecker, "Is New Urbanism Good for America?"

17. R. Steuteville, "Year of Growth for New Urbanism," *New Urban News,* September/October 1998, p. 1.

18. R. Henderson and A.T. Moore, "Plan Obsolescence," *Reason,* June 1998, pp. 42–47.

19. A. Krieger, "Whose Urbanism?" *Architecture,* November 1998, pp. 73–77.

20. Ibid., p. 75.

21. See Fulton, *The New Urbanism,* and M. Southworth, "Walkable Suburbs? An Evaluation of Neotraditional Communities at the Urban Edge," *Journal of the American Planning Association,* vol. 63, no. 1 (1997), pp. 28–44.

22. See J. Constantine, "Market Research: Survey of Homebuyers Shows Interest in Traditional Neighborhood Development," *Land Development,* Winter 1994, pp. 5–7.

23. J. Schleimer, "Case Study: Are Neo-Traditional Communities Succeeding in the Marketplace?" *Lusk Review,* Fall 1995, pp. 76–82.

24. P. Langdon, *A Better Place to Live* (Amherst, Mass.: Univ. of Massachusetts Press, 1994), p. 123.

Selecting the best new urbanist developments for this study

According to the September/October 1998 issue of New Urban News, *more than 200 new urbanist projects were in the planning stage or under construction in the United States as of September 1998. For this study, only a small number of communities representing the most complete examples of new urbanist developments were selected based on a series of quantitative and qualitative factors. Moreover, the statistical analysis depended on an adequate number of sales transactions in the surrounding conventional developments. This chapter presents the step-by-step process used to select the communities analyzed in the study.*

New Urbanist Developments In the United States

The first step in selecting communities was to identify the communities that maintain new urbanist characteristics. The most comprehensive list of new urbanist developments in the United States is found in *New Urban News*, which began the survey of new urbanist communities in the United States in 1996.[1] While it cannot be confirmed that *New Urban News* includes all new urbanist developments in the planning stage or beyond, the authors are confident that the best examples of new urbanist developments are included in this list.

New Urban News defines new urbanist developments as projects with "a mix of uses and housing types, interconnected network of streets, town center, formal civic spaces and squares, residential areas,

and pedestrian-oriented design."[2] All developments that meet *New Urban News*'s standards for new urbanist projects are listed in Figure 3-1. With advice from CNU's board members and staff at ULI, this list of 135 developments was narrowed to the six included in the study.

Choosing Communities for The Study Based on Quantitative Factors

The total number of developments listed in Figure 3-1 (from the September/October 1997 issue of *New Urban News*) was reduced for purely mechanical reasons. To perform meaningful regression analysis, a sufficient number of sales must occur in both the new urbanist development and in the surrounding area.[3] The minimum number of sales

Figure 3-1
New Urbanist Projects in the United States, 1997

Development*	Location	Acres	Designer
Alabama			
Blount Springs	Blount Springs	5,000	DPZ
Gorham's Bluff	Pisgah	186	Lloyd Vogt
Grangemoor	Montgomery	1,800	DPZ
The Ledges	Huntsville	—	UDA
Tannin	Orange Beach	60	DPZ
Arizona			
Civano	Tucson	820	Moule/Polyzoides DPZ, Wayne Moody
Monte Vista	Mesa	80	DPZ
Arkansas			
Brodie Creek	Little Rock	700	Nelessen Associates
Har-Ber Meadows	Spring Dale	425	EDI Architecture
California			
Bay Meadows Specific Plan	San Mateo	75	Calthorpe
Bernal Property	Pleasanton	510	Calthorpe
Capital River Park	Sacramento	52	Calthorpe
Colma Station Plan	Dale City	65	Calthorpe
Communications Hill	San Jose	500	Solomon
Courtside Village	Santa Rosa	68	Alan B. Cohen
The Crossings	Mountain View	16	Calthorpe
Curtis Park West	Sacramento	96	Lionakis-Beaumont
Del Paso Nuevo	Sacramento	150	Vail Engineering
Hillside Village	Petaluma	123	Calthorpe
Hughes-Fullerton Reuse Plan	Fullerton	270	Calthorpe
Jackson-Taylor	San Jose	75	Calthorpe
Laguna West	Sacramento County	1,033	Calthorpe
Loomis Town Center	Loomis	490	Calthorpe
Malibu Civic Center	Malibu	100	Calthorpe
Mountain Avenue Action Plan	Ontario	55	Calthorpe
Navel Center Reuse Plan	San Diego	380	MW Steele & Assoc., Rick Engineering
Petaluma Boulevard Neighborhood	Petaluma	18	Calthorpe
Playa Vista	Los Angeles	1,087	Moule/Polyzoides, DPZ
Rio Vista West	San Diego	95	Calthorpe
South Brentwood Village	Brentwood	140	Calthorpe
Suisun City Redevelopment	Suisun City	100	Roma Design Group
Colorado			
Elitch Gardens	Denver	30	Calthorpe
Dakota Ridge	Boulder	50	Calthorpe
Mill Village	Longmont	80	Swift and Associates
Prospect	Longmont	80	DPZ
Sherwood Villages	Weld County	397	Swift and Associates
Stapleton Redevelopment	Denver	500	Cooper/Robertson
Sunrise Creek	Montrose	62	Jim Burleigh
Florida			
Abacoa	Jupiter	2,100	DPZ, Calthorpe, Moule/Polyzoides
Amelia Park	Fernandina Beach	100	DPZ
Avalon Park	Orlando	1,860	DPZ
Celebration	Osceola County	4,900	Cooper/Robertson Robert A.M. Stern
Fallschase	Tallahassee	600	DPZ
Haile Plantation North	Gainesville	545	Robert Kramer and Matthew Kaskel

Development*	Location	Acres	Designer
Haile Village Center	Gainesville	50	Robert Kramer and Matthew Kaskel
Jordan Commons	Princeton	40	DPZ and others
Longleaf	New Port Richey	568	Geoffrey Farrell, Armando Montero
New Village	Kendall	100	Dover/Kohl
Orlando Naval Training Center	Orlando	1,133	Nelessen Associates
Rosemary Beach	Walton County	100	DPZ
Seaside	Walton County	80	DPZ
Silver Oaks Village	Zephyrhills	40	Community Planning & Research
Southeast Orlando	Orlando	12,000	Calthorpe
Southlake	Orlando	617	DPZ
Town of Tioga	Gainesville	280	Orjan Wetterqvist
West Kendall Project	Dade County	160	DPZ
Windsor	Vero Beach	400	DPZ
Georgia			
Riverside	Atlanta	70	DPZ
Illinois			
Centennial Crossing	Vernon Hills	110	Land Planning Services
Fox Mill (The Settlement)	Campen Township	100	Land Planning Services, Jim Spear
Mill Creek Village Center	Geneva	75	Dave Yocca, Design Workshop
Oswego Village Square	Oswego	85	Bucher-Willis
Town Center Plan	Plainfield	300	Richard Schaupp, Michael Franck
Indiana			
Beachwalk	Michigan City	106	Allegretti Architects
Kentucky			
Norton Commons	Louisville	600	DPZ
Park DuValle	Louisville	100	UDA
Maryland			
Clarksburg Town Center	Montgomery County	275	CHK
Kentlands	Gaithersburg	352	DPZ
King Farm	Montgomery County	440	CHK
Lafayette Courts	Baltimore	21	CHK
Lakelands	Gaithersburg	343	DPZ
Lexington Terrace	Baltimore	18	CHK
St. James	Prince Georges County	430	Nelessen Associates
Sandtown-Winchester	Baltimore	100	UDA
Sandy Spring	Sandy Spring	400	DPZ
Massachusetts			
Churchill Neighborhood Plan	Holyoke	40	Calthorpe
Mashpee Commons	Mashpee	294	DPZ
Michigan			
Clinton Valley Center	Pontiac	437	Oakland County
Mayfield Park	Mayfield Township	105	Gibbs Planning Group
Shelby Town Center	Shelby Township	120	Gibbs Planning Group
Stonelea	Highland Township	850	DPZ
Mississippi			
Colfax Village	West Point	40	Geoffrey Ferrell and Suzanne Askey Lauter
Cotton District	Starkville	—	Dan Camp
Missouri			
Wildwood Town Center	Wildwood	1,200	DPZ

continued

Figure 3-1 *(continued)*

New Urbanist Projects in the United States, 1997

Development*	Location	Acres	Designer
New Jersey			
Town Center Plan	Washington Township	700	Nelessen Associates
New Mexico			
Frijoles	Santa Fe	344	DPZ
New York			
General Motors Site	Sleepy Hollow	96	Cooper, Robertson
North Carolina			
First Ward Master Plan	Charlotte	134	UDA
New Village	Huntersville	239	DPZ
Primrose Beach	Currituk	85	Melanie Taylor
Ramah	Huntersville	70	DPZ
Southern Village	Chapel Hill	350	Doug Stimmel
Trillium	Cashiers	650	DPZ
Vermillion	Huntersville	300	DPZ
Village of Woodsong	Shallotte	22	Thomas Low
Ohio			
Adams Landing	Cincinnati	30	DPZ
Neighborhoods of Central	Cleveland	360	DPZ, City Architecture, UDA
Oregon			
Canyon Rim Neighborhood	Redmond	95	Lennertz Coyle
Fairview Village	Fairview	88	Lennertz Coyle, William Dennis
Greenhill Village	Eugene	80	Community Planning & Research
LeGrande Neighborhood	LeGrande	20	Lennertz Coyle
McKenzie	Springfield	100	Lennertz Coyle
North Mountain Neighborhood	Ashland	58	Lennertz Coyle
Old Mill District	Bend	250	Ken-Kay Associates
Shevlin Riverfront	Bend	19	Lennertz Coyle
Sunnyside Village	Clackamas County	278	Calthorpe
Pennsylvania			
Charmbury	Hanover	150	TCA
Eagleview	Uwchlan Township	150	Hankin Group
Hill District	Pittsburgh	80	UDA
Livable Communities Project	Lancaster	50	Gene Aleci, TCA
Nine Mile Run	Pittsburgh	225	Cooper, Robertson
Pennwood	Morgantown	173	TCA
South Carolina			
Clear Springs	Fort Mill	4,800	LandDesign Inc.
Daniel Island	Charleston	3,800	Cooper, Robertson, J. Barnett, DPZ
Habersham Village	Beaufort County	275	DPZ
I'On	Mount Pleasant	243	DPZ, Dover/Kohl DesignWorks Seamon, Whiteside
New Market	Greenwood	30	DPZ
Newpoint	Beaufort County	54	Cowart/Graham
Port Royal	Beaufort County	—	Dover/Kohl
Tennessee			
Cordova, the Town	East Memphis	55	Looney Ricks Kiss, Fisher & Arnold
Harbor Town	Memphis	110	RTKL Associates
Mid-Town Corridor	Memphis	56	City of Memphis
Schilling Farms	Collierville	446	Looney Ricks Kiss, Fisher & Arnold
South Bluffs	Memphis	35	RTKL Associates

Development*	Location	Acres	Designer
Texas			
Addison Circle	Addison	80	RTKL Associates
Beachtown	Galveston	221	DPZ
Utah			
Wolf Mountain	Park City	300	DPZ
Virginia			
Belmont Forest	Loudoun County	273	DPZ
Brambleton	Loudoun County	2,500	CHK
East Ocean View	Norfolk	100	DPZ
Haymount	Caroline County	1,682	DPZ
New Town in James City County	Williamsburg	600	Cooper, Robertson
Warrington Hall	Chesapeake	127	Porterfield Design
Washington			
Northwest Landing	Du Pont	3,000	Calthorpe
Wisconsin			
Middleton Hills	Madison	149	DPZ

*Projects generally include a mix of uses and housing types, interconnected network of streets, town center, formal civic spaces and squares, residential areas, and pedestrian-oriented design.
Source: *New Urban News*, September/October 1997, pp. 10–13.

necessary to complete a meaningful pricing analysis is based on the number of factors that are used to explain the sale price. A statistical rule of thumb is that the number of sales must be at least five times larger than the number of explanatory attributes included in the model.[4] The pricing models used in the analysis include approximately 30 housing attributes; therefore, the minimum number of single-family house transaction records required for the regression is approximately 150. Figure 3-2 lists the 12 new urbanist communities that had at least 150 housing units completed as of the September/October 1997 issue of *New Urban News*.

Figure 3-2

New Urbanist Developments with More Than 150 Completed Units

Development	Location	Units Completed	Total Acreage
Celebration	Osceola County, FL	560	4,900
The Crossings	Mountain View, CA	270	16
Harbor Town	Memphis, TN	410	110
Hill District	Pittsburgh, PA	230	80
Kentlands	Gaithersburg, MD	1,275	352
Laguna West	Sacramento County, CA	990	1,033
Northwest Landing	Du Pont, WA	225	3,000
Seaside	Walton County, FL	300	80
South Bluffs	Memphis, TN	280*	35
Southern Village	Chapel Hill, NC	180	350
Southlake	Orlando, FL	240*	617
Sunnyside Village	Clackamas County, OR	350	278

*A majority of completed units are multifamily housing. Therefore, the development was excluded from the analysis.
Source: *New Urban News*, September/October 1997, pp. 10–13.

Among the 12 communities, Southlake in Orlando, Florida, and South Bluffs in Memphis, Tennessee, contain a majority of multifamily units and so were not included in the analysis. The remaining ten developments were expected to provide a sufficient number of sales of single-family residences from 1994 to 1997 to complete a quantitative analysis of new urbanist and conventional developments.

Choosing Communities for The Study Based on Qualitative Factors

Several communities were excluded for qualitative reasons. Three qualitative factors, urban redevelopment, municipally funded projects, and resort communities, were used to further pare the list.

Urban Redevelopment

One limitation of studying urban redevelopment projects is that the areas surrounding an urban revitalization project may have characteristics similar to those of the new urbanist development under study. If the area surrounding an urban redevelopment project has the same characteristics as the new urbanist development, the pricing model is unable to capture the price differential between new urbanist and conventional communities. The Hill District project in Pittsburgh, Pennsylvania, and the Crossings in Mountain View, California, were excluded for this reason.

Municipal Projects

Sale prices of houses in municipally subsidized projects may not reflect the true market value of the properties. If all units in a municipally developed project are subsidized, the effect of the government subsidy may be difficult, if not impossible, to separate from attributes of the housing resulting from the new urbanism. Therefore, the price differential between properties in a municipally developed new urbanist community and housing units in the surrounding area is likely to be biased. For this reason, Sunnyside Village in Clackamas County, Oregon, was excluded from the analysis.

Resort Communities

Several new urbanist projects are resort communities, and a portion of the residents in these communities have purchased a second home or a vacation home. Resort communities generally offer a different set of amenities to residents and may attract a different clientele from year-round developments. Prices for a second home in a resort area may not be comparable with other developments that house year-round residents. Therefore, resort communities were excluded from the study, eliminating Seaside, Florida, from the analysis. Figure 3-3 shows the list of remaining new urbanist developments

Figure 3-3
New Urbanist Developments That Meet Both Quantitative And Qualitative Selection Criteria

Development	Developer	Location	Year Opened
Kentlands	Great Seneca Development Corp.	Gaithersburg, MD	1990
Harbor Town	Henry Turley Co.	Memphis, TN	1990
Laguna West	AKT Development Corp.	Sacramento County, CA	1991
Southern Village	Bryan Properties, Inc.	Chapel Hill, NC	1994
Northwest Landing*	Weyerhaeuser Real Estate Co.	Du Pont, WA	1995
Celebration*	The Celebration Company	Osceola County, FL	1996

*Later removed from the list because of a lack of comparable housing in the immediate neighborhood.

that maintain a minimum number of sales and meet a series of qualitative tests. This final list of developments includes the most often cited new urbanist developments in the literature (Seaside excepted): Kentlands, Harbor Town, Laguna West, Southern Village, Northwest Landing, and Celebration.[5] The authors visited each of these new urbanist developments to assess the viability of the community and its comparability with surrounding conventional developments.

Notes

1. Lists of such projects were published in May/June 1996, November/December 1996, September/October 1997, and September/October 1998.
2. "Traditional Neighborhood Development Projects in the U.S.," *New Urban News,* September/October 1997, p. 10.
3. A complete discussion of the quantitative methods used to isolate the effect of the new urbanism is presented in Chapter 5.
4. See J.F. Hair, R.E. Anderson, R.L. Tatham, and W.C. Black, *Multivariate Data Analysis,* 4th ed. (Englewood Cliffs, N.J.: Prentice-Hall, 1995), p. 105.
5. Northwest Landing and Celebration were later removed from the list because of a lack of comparable housing units in the immediate neighborhood.

Descriptions of the selected communities

This chapter describes the new urbanist communities selected for the study. Each description includes location, community plan, current development status, new urbanist characteristics, a regional map, and a site plan.

Kentlands

Kentlands is a 352-acre project in Gaithersburg, Maryland, 13 miles northwest of Washington, D.C. (Figures 4-1 and 4-2). The original master plan for Kentlands included 1,600 dwelling units, 1 million square feet of office space, and 1.2 million square feet of retail space.[1] As of late 1998, 1,200 housing units and 335,000 square feet of retail space had been completed.[2] Other facilities include an elementary school, a clubhouse, a daycare center, and a church. Because of the excess supply of office space in the region, the office component of the development has been postponed.

Sited on the historic Kent Farm tract, Kentlands includes a variety of public open spaces, which cover approximately 28 percent of the development. A wetland preserve, greenbelts, and small town squares help to define individual neighborhoods, and each neighborhood has a distinctive character. For example, the Old Farm neighborhood surrounds the original Kent homestead, which currently serves as the town's cultural arts center, while the Hill District, centered around a community clubhouse, overlooks the Old Farm and the wetlands. Kentlands includes single-family detached houses, townhouses, condominiums, apartments, and carriage houses (units built over garages).

Streets in Kentlands are laid out in an interconnected pattern with some loops because of the topography. The exterior appearance of the housing units in Kentlands is markedly different from that in surrounding conventional subdivisions: houses are designed with white picket fences and front porches, and alleys at the rear of each lot replace driveways and front-loading garages. A pedestrian-friendly environment was created by narrowing streets and providing sidewalks throughout the development. Local bus service through the community provides a link to a regional subway station.

Kentlands is one of the most cited new urbanist developments for its features: mixed housing types, interconnected streets, a pedestrian-friendly environment, and, in particular, its architectural design. Kentlands is not a perfect example of a new urbanist community, however. For example, because of its suburban location, most residents drive to work. Because of its size and the position

Figure 4-1
Regional Map of the Washington, D.C., Area

Figure 4-2
Site Plan of Kentlands

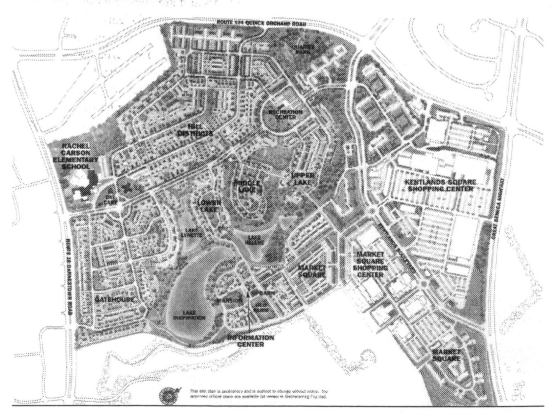

of its retail component, most housing units are more than a five-minute walk from the retail shops. Nevertheless, Kentlands represents one of the earliest and best examples of new urbanist development.

Harbor Town

Harbor Town is located on Mud Island, an island surrounded by the Mississippi and Wolf Rivers and adjacent to Memphis, Tennessee's central business district (Figures 4-3 and 4-4). The community's location is easily accessible to downtown Memphis, but, because it is on an island, it is also self-contained. On a 110-acre site, Harbor Town is planned for 850 dwelling units, a town square, a school, and a marina. As of late 1998, about 300 single-family detached houses, 30 rowhouses and duplexes, and 350 apartments had been completed.

Harbor Town's street grid is intersected by several diagonal boulevards, which help define the three neighborhoods in the development. The Harbor District of Harbor Town contains the community's commercial components, a marina, and high-density residential development, which includes both garden apartments and apartments above commercial space. Commercial uses include a grocery store, small specialty shops, and office space. A private school serving children up to eighth grade is also located in this district. The Garden District includes a mix of detached and attached housing units integrated with parks, ponds, and a nature trail. The Village District is a densely configured residential neighborhood with a mix of apartments, townhouses, and detached single-family houses.

Harbor Town offers a variety of open spaces, including parks, a wooded area, trails, and ponds. Residents use public space for recreational purposes and as a gathering spot for social activities. Residents have easy access to the Green Belt Park along the Mississippi River at the western edge of the development. The community provides a walkable environment: most houses have front porches and short setbacks, garages are entered from the rear of lots and are connected by alleys, and there are sidewalks and plenty of trees.

As one of the early new urbanist projects and therefore one of the most complete examples of new urbanist communities, Harbor Town is almost built out. Currently the community has no public schools, only a private Montessori school. Because of its unique location, children cannot walk or ride bikes to public schools, and public transit is not available on the island.

Figure 4-3
Regional Map of the Memphis Area

Figure 4-4
Site Plan of Harbor Town

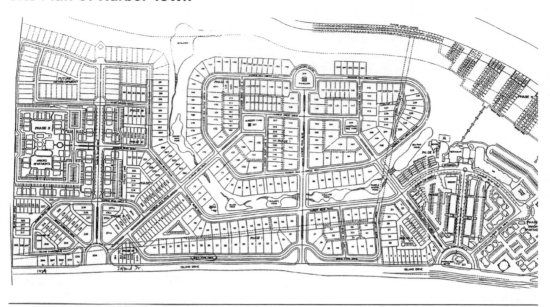

Laguna West

Laguna West is built on a former rice paddy in Elk Grove, California, approximately 12 miles south of downtown Sacramento (Figures 4-5 and 4-6). The Elk Grove area has been intensively developed in recent years. Most new developments in the area are conventional subdivisions; Laguna West is the only community designed with new urbanist principles.

Laguna West is planned for a mixed-use community, with 2,000 single-family houses, 1,200 multifamily units, retail space, offices, and light industrial space. In addition to approximately 600 single-family housing units, Laguna West also has a day-care center, a church, a retail market, and an elementary school that is scheduled to open fall 1999. A housing complex for senior citizens was completed in 1998, but proposed condominiums and apartments have not been built to date. Apple Computer and JVC Corp. have built offices and manufacturing facilities in the development.

Unlike Kentlands and Harbor Town, whose architectural design is clearly different from the surrounding area, the exteriors of houses in Laguna West are designed in the contemporary style similar to other subdivisions in the Elk Grove area. What differentiates Laguna West from nearby conventional subdivisions are its public space and pedestrian-friendly environment. The entire community is developed around a 73-acre artificial lake. Adjacent to the lake is Town Square Park, which features a basketball court, playground, and rose garden. Also located in the park is the Laguna Town Hall, which has a multipurpose room that can accommodate 500 people, and an outdoor amphitheater. The Town Hall, managed by the Elk Grove Community Services District, serves the entire Elk Grove area. The development also has a few neighborhood parks, off-street paths, and on-street bikeways.

A pedestrian-friendly environment is not consistently available in Laguna West. For example, alleys and rear-entrance garages are available in only a small section; in some areas, garages are placed at the rear of the site and connected with long driveways, and in other areas, the view of garage

Figure 4-5
Regional Map of the Sacramento Area

doors dominates the street-scape. Another problem is the slow development of the condominium and apartment units. Multifamily components, which are located between the town center and single-family areas, are still in the planning stage. As a result, numerous empty lots stand between completed housing units and the center of activities, making it an unfriendly environment for pedestrians.

Laguna West was originally designed to be a major stop of a regional light-rail system, but unfortunately, the transit system is unlikely to be completed in the near future.

Figure 4-6
Site Plan of Laguna West

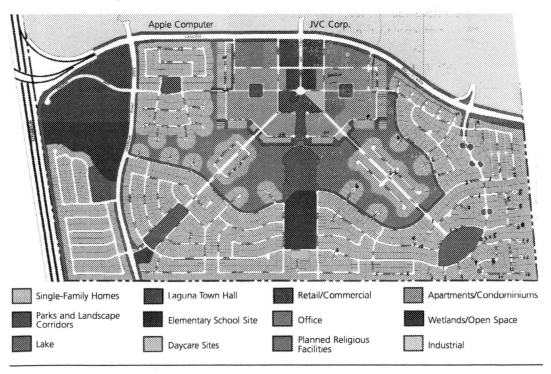

Single-Family Homes	Laguna Town Hall	Retail/Commercial	Apartments/Condominiums
Parks and Landscape Corridors	Elementary School Site	Office	Wetlands/Open Space
Lake	Daycare Sites	Planned Religious Facilities	Industrial

Southern Village

Southern Village is sited at the southern edge of the city of Chapel Hill, North Carolina, along Highway 15-501 (Figures 4-7 and 4-8).[3] This development includes a village center and seven neighborhoods. Upon completion, Southern Village will have approximately 1,250 dwelling units, 20 acres of commercial space, and 114 acres of open space and recreational facilities. As of late 1998, approximately 200 single-family houses and 20 town-houses had been completed.

The village center, which was under construction as of

Figure 4-7
Regional Map of the Chapel Hill Area

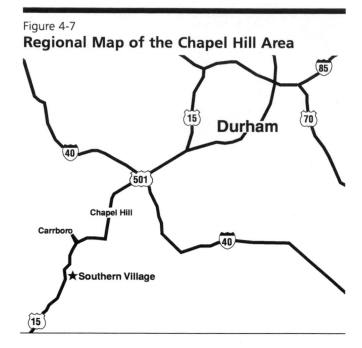

Figure 4-8
Site Plan of Southern Village

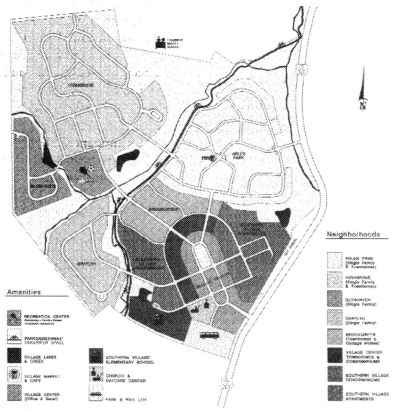

late 1998, is the primary site of Southern Village's nonresidential components. Upon completion, the center will have office space, a variety of retail stores, and a movie theater. Also sited at the center are a church and a daycare facility. Residential neighborhoods surrounding the village center offer high-density housing units, such as apartments and condominiums; farther away from the center are townhouses and single-family housing.

Open space and recreational facilities occupy approximately 35 percent of the site. Amenities include a recreation center, jogging/biking trails, small ponds, and village parks. Because of the irregular topography, streets in the community are not laid out on a grid; nevertheless, culs-de-sac are avoided. Southern Village also encourages walking, with its narrow streets, tree-lined sidewalks, rear alleys, and houses with short setbacks and front porches. When the Southern Village Elementary School opens in 1999, children in the community will be able to walk to school.

A shortcoming of Southern Village at the moment is the lack of retail space. Despite the community's walkable environment, residents still need to drive to nearby shopping centers. As the town center and the elementary school are completed, however, Southern Village will embody the true spirit of the new urbanism.

Northwest Landing

Northwest Landing is located in the city of Du Pont, Washington, midway between Tacoma and Olympia along I-5 (Figures 4-9 and 4-10). Du Pont has two neighborhoods—the historic turn-of-the-century village and Northwest Landing. A 300-foot greenbelt serves as a buffer between the two neighborhoods. Currently, approximately 1,000 people live in Northwest Landing, about 600 in the historic village. Upon completion in 2025, Northwest Landing will be a 3,000-acre community providing homes for 10,000 people and jobs for 8,600 people.

The master plan for Northwest Landing includes residential units, schools, retail space, offices, and manufacturing plants. The residential area will have four villages. Village I, with approximately 520 dwelling units, is almost complete. Housing includes single-family houses in a wide range of sizes and prices, condominiums, and apartments. In 1995, the first business began operation in Northwest Landing; today four major corporations—State Farm Insurance, Intel, Lone Star Northwest, and Westblock Pacific—are located in the community. The integration of residential units and employment centers provides jobs close enough for residents to walk or bicycle to work. The developer anticipates that at least 30 percent of Northwest Landing's future population will work at companies located in the community.

Northwest Landing embraces many new urbanist features that enhance walkability. Streets are interconnected, houses are placed close to the street and many have

Figure 4-9
Regional Map of the Tacoma Area

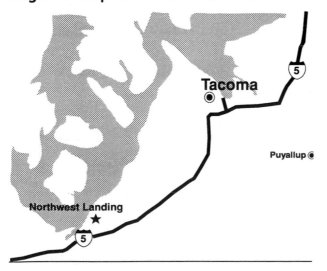

Figure 4-10
Site Plan of Northwest Landing

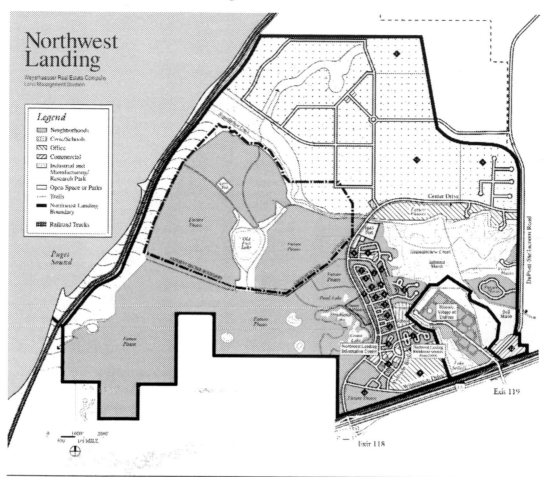

front porches, garages are to the rear of the lots and served by alleys, and tree-lined streets and sidewalks enhance the community's walkability.

At its current stage of development, however, residents experience some inconveniences. For example, the city of Du Pont does not have sufficient retail outlets, so residents must drive several miles to pick up groceries and other necessities. No schools have been built in the community, although two are in the development plan, and the nearest school is six miles away. When completed in 2025, however, Northwest Landing is expected to be an integrated, pedestrian-friendly community.

Celebration

Celebration is a 4,900-acre community developed by the Celebration Company, a subsidiary of the Walt Disney Company. Located just south of the EPCOT Center near Orlando, Florida (Figures 4-11 and 4-12), the development has four residential villages: Celebration Village, West Village, Lake Evalyn, and North Village. A total of 764 single-family homes, 72 townhouses, and 123 apartments are planned. In addition to the residential component, Celebration includes a health care facility, a 109-acre office park with 1 million square feet of space, a teaching academy, a public school serving

Figure 4-11
Regional Map of the Kissimmee Area

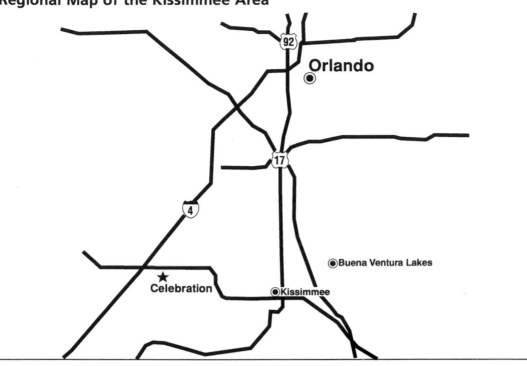

Figure 4-12
Site Plan of Celebration

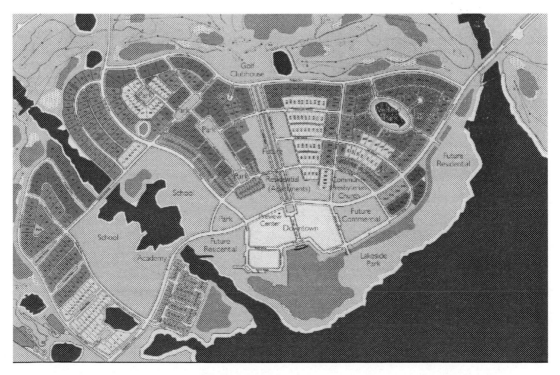

kindergarten through 12th grade, a golf course, and a downtown.

The downtown area is designed as a Main Street of a traditional town and includes a town hall, bank, post office, cinema, retail shops, restaurants, lakeside promenade, and apartment buildings. The phasing of Celebration is different from other new urbanist communities. While most new urbanist projects build the residential component first and retail component later, Celebration completed its downtown area before completion of most residential areas. Across a small lake from downtown is Lakeside Park, where tennis courts, a swimming pool, and basketball and volleyball courts are available. Residents can also use the jogging and biking trails and small neighborhood parks scattered throughout the community for recreation. The scattered public spaces provide opportunities for residents to interact with neighbors and help create a sense of community.

Another important element of this development is Celebration School and Teaching Academy. The Osceola County School District operates and oversees Celebration's public school, which opened in fall 1996. The 36-acre campus is expected to accommodate 1,000 students. The location of the school allows children in Celebration to walk or bike to classes. The adjacent Teaching Academy explores new teaching methods and provides teacher training and curriculum development.

While Celebration contains many of the characteristics available in typical new urbanist developments, it also has a few unique features. For example, two community development districts, not the local government, provide funding for infrastructure and recreational amenities in Celebration.[4] A fiber-optic network providing interactive communications will link all homes in the community. The development also has an 18-hole golf course. Because of Celebration's many unusual features, it may be difficult to separate the impact of the new urbanism from the effects of these special features when compared with conventional developments.

Notes

1. A. Duany and E. Plater-Zyberk, *Towns and Town-Making Principles* (Cambridge, Mass.: Harvard Univ. Graduate School of Design, 1991), p. 52.

2. The 335,000-square-foot Kentlands Shopping Center was completed in 1992. The first store in Market Square, a 60,000-square-foot main street retail area, opened in late 1998.

3. Currently outside the city boundary of Chapel Hill, Southern Village is expected to be included in the city soon.

4. Osceola County provides police, fire, and emergency medical services.

Statistical methods of comparing home sale prices

CHAPTER 5

A simple and direct means of determining the price differential between new urbanist and conventional communities is to compare average sale prices for recent transactions. Figure 5-1 reveals that the average sale price in each of the new urbanist communities considered was higher than for the surrounding developments during 1994 to 1997. On average, consumers were willing to pay approximately $67,000 more (ranging from $18,000 to $162,000 more) to reside in a new urbanist development rather than a conventional suburban development.

Although comparing averages can be instructive, it can also be deceptive. Average price differentials between new urbanist developments and conventional suburban developments can be compared in a meaningful way if all other housing attributes are the same for both types of development. Attributes of new urbanist housing may differ from those of conventional housing, however, in ways that also affect the price of the home. Several differences might include lot size, quality of construction, and age and size of the house, to name a few. If these differences in attributes are not accounted for, a comparison of average home prices in new urbanist developments and conventional suburban developments could be deceptive.

To control for differentials in attributes, it is necessary to use more sophisticated statistical tools, one of which is regression analysis. Regression analysis provides a quan-

Figure 5-1

Comparison of Average Single-Family Home Prices, 1994–1997

	Average Sale Price	
Community	New Urbanist Development	Area Surrounding the New Urbanist Development
Kentlands	$294,280	$231,260
Harbor Town	204,340	92,120
Laguna West	166,110	141,230
Southern Village	240,410	217,180
Northwest Landing	160,970	142,620
Celebration	279,510	117,030

Data sources: First American Real Estate Solutions and Shelby County Assessor's Office.

titative tool to test the behavior of consumers when purchasing a single-family home. The application of regression to single-family housing valuation is referred to as the hedonic price model.[1] Consumer pricing behavior is tested using actual data in the regression equation. The results of regression analysis allow researchers, developers, planners, and appraisers to draw conclusions through statistical relationships. The Appraisal Institute recognizes the importance of regression analysis in the appraisal of single-family houses by dedicating 37 pages of its text to the subject.[2] The following paragraphs present an overview of regression analysis as applied to real estate valuation.

Estimating Single-Family Home Prices Using Regression Analysis

Regression analysis measures the relationship between one economic variable, the "dependent variable," and one or more explanatory variables, the "independent variables." The price of a single-family home (the dependent variable) is *dependent* on the attributes of that home (the independent variables). The value of each attribute or independent variable is determined by the utility that the consumer obtains by owning a home with that characteristic. Thus, the price of a single-family home can be explained by valuing each housing attribute.

In essence, regression allows us to measure the complex nature of consumer behavior when selecting a place to live. Intuitively, consumers place more value on an additional bathroom, a larger house, a new house, or the prestige of living in an upscale neighborhood. By looking at a relatively large sample of single-family home sales, we can determine the value differential between a three-bedroom house and a four-bedroom house, holding other attributes equal. Similarly, the value differential between a house located in a new urbanist community and one located in a conventional development can also be estimated.

If all consumers have the same opinion of the important attributes in a single-family home and each of these preferences can be measured, researchers would be able to pre-

dict the value of a single-family home with perfect accuracy. While the vast majority of prices for single-family houses are explained with regression models, consumers do not always have the same tastes, and not all consumer behavior is easily measured. For instance, an empty-nester household might place a different value on a large lot than a household with school-age children. Thus, the price of a single-family home is measured with some error.

Estimating sale prices of single-family homes is *dependent* on consumer behavior. Therefore, we need to determine the factors that are important when homebuyers select a house to purchase. Using data from 100 sales transactions in the 20878 zip code (the zip code that includes Kentlands), we graphically illustrate the relationship between the sale price of a home (on the y-axis or vertically) and the living area of the house (on the x-axis or horizontally).[3] Each dot in Figure 5-2 represents a sales transaction, and the cloud of dots represents the relationship between sale price and living area. Figure 5-2 reveals that consumers pay more for a house that has more interior living area. A straight line drawn through the middle of the plotted points slopes upward from left to right (Figure 5-3). If drawn correctly, this

Figure 5-2

Scatter Plot of Home Price Versus Living Area for 100 Kentlands Sales

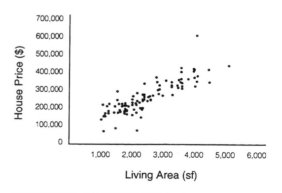

Figure 5-3
Scatter Plot of Home Price versus Living Area with Best Fit Line For 100 Kentlands Sales

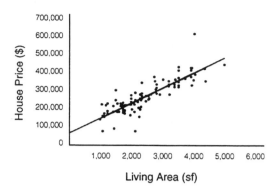

Figure 5-4
Best Fit Line for Simple Linear Regression

$$y = a + b \cdot x$$

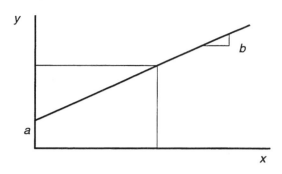

line represents the best estimate of the relationship between single-family sale prices and house size. The line would also represent the simple linear regression of house price as the dependent variable and living area as the independent variable.

Although house size does explain some portion of the house price, the lack of a tight distribution of plotted points around the line indicates that living area does not completely explain the price of a single-family home. If all the plotted points fell along the straight line, living area would explain all the variation in single-family sale prices and other housing attributes would be unnecessary to explain single-family sale prices (see Figure 5-4). Because there is a cloud of plotted points around the straight line in Figure 5-3, other factors affect single-family house prices that need to be included in the analysis.

Multiple regression allows for two or more independent variables to simultaneously affect the value of single-family homes. A second independent variable, say number of bathrooms, can be added to the regression model to better explain sale prices for single-family homes. Graphically, this can be explained with a three-dimensional graph, where the number of bathrooms is placed

on the z-axis (see Figure 5-5). The three-dimensional cloud that would be created reveals the results of a multiple regression analysis where living area and number of bathrooms explain prices for single-family homes. By including the number of bathrooms in the regression analysis, more of the variation in home prices is explained by the model. One of the limitations of graphing multiple regression results is that more than two independent variables cannot be plotted against single-family sale prices. It is necessary, however, to include more than

Figure 5-5
Best Fit Line for Multiple Linear Regression with Two Independent Variables

$$y = a + b_1 \cdot x + b_2 \cdot z$$

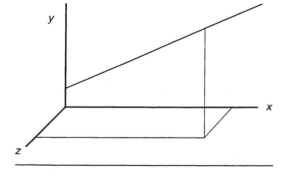

house area and number of bathrooms in a regression explaining single-family sale prices, as consumers value more than these two attributes. To assess the validity of the relationship between single-family sale prices and multiple independent variables, more complex statistical ratios must be understood.

Important Statistics in Regression Analysis

The validity of a multiple regression analysis relies heavily on three ratios. First, the overall credibility of a regression model is measured using the F-statistic. Second, the explanatory power of the regression model is ascertained by the R-squared. Third, the t-statistic determines whether a particular independent variable provides unique explanatory power to the regression model.

F-Statistic

The F-statistic measures the likelihood that results of a regression model are attributable to chance. In other words, the F-statistic measures the probability that the relationship between the dependent variable and the independent variables can be attributed to luck; the higher the F-statistic, the less likely the relationship is attributable to luck.[4] For the house price regressions in this case, an F-statistic of greater than 4.00 is significant at the 99 percent level,[5] meaning that there is a 99 percent level of certainty that the relationship in the multiple regression model is not attributable to a chance relationship.

R-Squared

R-squared measures the proportion of the variation that is explained by the regression model. R-squared values have a range of 0 to 100 percent, but these extremes are seldom achieved. The higher the R-squared, the better the explanatory power of the model. The complexity of economic decisions and consumer behavior prevents most models that explain single-family house prices from achieving an explanatory power of greater than 95 percent. Instead, the R-squared of most single-family house price models ranges from 80 to 95 percent.

t-Statistic

The t-statistic measures the importance of individual independent variables in a regression analysis. As a rule of thumb, t-statistics of greater than 2.0 or less than −2.0 indicate that an independent variable provides explanatory power (at the 95 percent level of confidence) in estimating the dependent variable. Additionally, it is important to note the relationship of the independent variable with the dependent variable. For instance, if the house size is not positively related to house price, the analyst should ask why a larger house is worth less money. If there is not a good rationale for this situation, the results of the regression should be called into question.

Types of Economic Relationships

Simple linear regression assumes that one variable (the independent variable) can predict a second variable (the dependent variable) and that the relationship is a straight line (see Figure 5-6). Most economic relationships maintain a nonlinear relationship, however. The relationship

Figure 5-6
Graph of Constant Returns-to-Scale

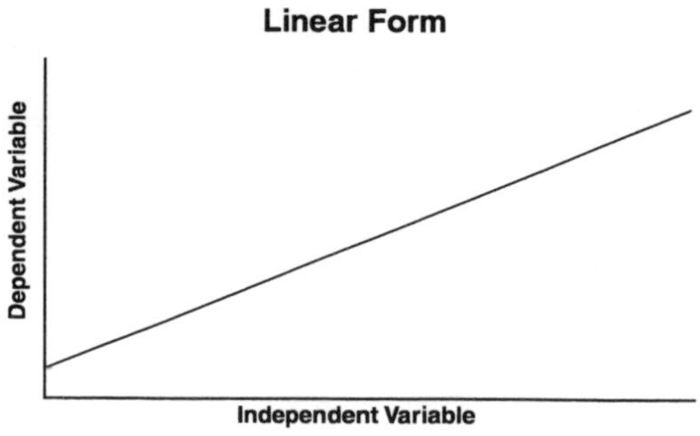

Linear Form

between the dependent and independent variables does not need to be linear in regression analyses.

An economic relationship can take a variety of forms. The most common economic relationship is referred to as diminishing returns-to-scale. Using a common example, a second scoop of ice cream on an ice cream cone is not worth as much as the first scoop, the third scoop is worth less than the second scoop, and at some point your utility or enjoyment of an additional scoop of ice cream is of no greater benefit (assuming that you have no ability to keep the ice cream frozen). Thus, your enjoyment is less for every additional scoop until an additional scoop is virtually worthless.

Diminishing returns-to-scale are most commonly graphed using a semi-log form as shown in Figure 5-7. Note in Figure 5-7 that for every additional unit of the independent variable (i.e., scoops of ice cream), the dependent variable (i.e., consumer enjoyment) increases but at a decreasing rate. An analogous example would be the enjoyment of an additional square foot of lot. Each additional square foot of lot is worth slightly less than the prior square foot in many housing markets.

Another economic relationship is an increasing returns-to-scale, which is the converse of decreasing returns-to-scale. Each

Figure 5-7
Graph of Diminishing Returns-to-Scale
Semi-Log Form

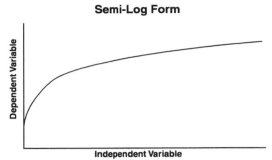

additional unit of the dependent variable is worth more than the previous unit. As presented in Figure 5-8, increasing returns-to-scale are sometimes used to explain the agglomeration benefits of many retailers' locating close to each other. As the number of retailers increases (the independent variable), retail sales per square foot increase (the dependent variable). Increasing returns-to-scale are not frequently found in consumer behavior, but retailing is one area where increasing returns-to-scale may exist.

A third possible relationship is referred to as a quadratic relationship or changing returns-to-scale relationship. A good example of a quadratic relationship is the effect of a house's age on its value. In the first decades

Figure 5-8
Graph of Increasing Returns-to-Scale
Exponential Form

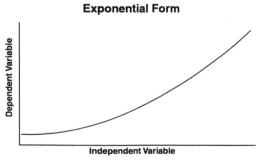

Figure 5-9
Graph of Changing Returns-to-Scale
Quadratic Form

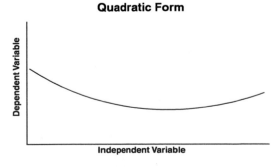

of a house's life, its relative value may depreciate as a result of physical and functional obsolescence. As time goes on, however, the effects of the obsolescence may be reversed by renovation, and consumers' preferences may change. Figure 5-9 graphically depicts the quadratic effect of age on the value of a home. In the early years, the value of the house decreases until it reaches a point where its value begins to rise with age. The quadratic form is a combination of the linear and increasing returns-to-scale relationships.

While regression analyses involve a range of complex economic relationships, the results of such analyses allow researchers and practitioners to draw explanatory conclusions from these statistical relationships. Hedonic price models apply regression to the proposed economic relationship between housing amenities and price. In hedonic price models, housing is viewed as a bundle of goods, including site, improvement, location, and market characteristics.

Notes

1. See the appendix for an academic discussion of the hedonic price model. Throughout the remainder of this book, "regression" and "hedonic pricing" are used interchangeably.

2. See Appraisal Institute, *The Appraisal of Real Estate,* 11th ed. (Chicago: Appraisal Institute, 1996).

3. Although it is possible to plot 2,392 transactions in a single scatter plot, the large number of observations reveals a relatively meaningless solid black cloud.

4. Suggesting that the *F*-statistic simply measures whether the significance of the model is attributable to luck is a gross simplification. For a detailed discussion of the usefulness of the *F*-statistic, see J.F. Hair, R.E. Anderson, R.L. Tatham, and W.C. Black, *Multivariate Data Analysis,* 4th ed. (Englewood Cliffs, N.J.: Prentice-Hall, 1995), p. 119.

5. The exact value depends on both the number of explanatory variables and the number of observations in the regression model. Given the set of explanatory variables and a large number of home sale records used in the study, critical value is approximately 2.

6

Attributes of single-family housing

CHAPTER 6

This chapter presents the facts or data used to test the theory that was presented in the first five chapters.

To estimate the value that consumers place on new urbanist communities, a complete and high-quality data set is necessary. The quantitative methods used to analyze the data require information on transaction prices as well as the housing attributes that homebuyers find important in their decisions to buy housing. Without a high-quality data set, it may be difficult, if not impossible, to draw reasonable conclusions from the quantitative findings. This chapter presents the collected information for each new urbanist community considered and the areas surrounding them. In addition to discussing the sales transactions and housing attributes for each community and for the combined data set, individual sales transactions that were eliminated are described and the reason for their removal discussed. After examination of the data on single-family home transactions, Northwest Landing and Celebration were removed from the final list of communities because of the lack of sales of comparable properties in the adjacent areas.

Data Sources

All data used in this study were provided by secondary sources, so that other researchers can replicate the findings. The primary data source for the study came from the property data files compiled by First American Real Estate Solutions (FARES, formerly known as Experian), a real estate information provider. FARES collects, compiles, and distributes information on single-family properties in 35 states. All data were collected using FARES's online system. Each property record includes the property's legal identification, assessor's parcel number (APN), property location, and assessed value, as well as information on the most recent sale price and dozens of site and property improvement attributes. Using the APN for each property, the FARES data were combined with data collected from other sources.

One important property attribute that FARES does not maintain is the construction quality of the improvements. Data about the quality of property construction were collected from the Maryland State Department of Assessment and Taxation, the Orange County (North Carolina) Tax Office, and the Osceola County (Florida) Property Appraiser. These data were then merged with the FARES property data. FARES's property data covered all selected new urbanist communities except Harbor Town. As a result, data for the analysis of Harbor Town came from the 1998 Certified Roll provided by the Shelby County (Tennessee) Assessor's Office.

Property Attributes

For a regression model to accurately estimate the price of a single-family home, housing attributes that are important to consumers' decisions about purchasing housing must be included in the model. As such, this study attempts to include as many housing attributes as are consistently provided by FARES in each of the new urbanist communities and in the surrounding housing markets.[1] If certain housing attributes were not included in the model and were important to consumers' decisions to purchase housing, the model could have "missing variable bias." While no model can ever capture all aspects of consumers' behavior, this study attempts to be as thorough as possible and to be without prejudice on which housing attributes may or may not be important to consumers in purchasing decisions.

Housing markets vary in different parts of the United States to meet the needs and desires of consumers; therefore, the data collected by municipal governments and housing data suppliers were not uniform across communities. As municipalities maintain different sets of housing characteristics in the assessor's rolls, the resulting set of housing attributes collected by FARES varies from community to community. While specific attributes may differ by com-

munity (e.g., types of roofing material and exterior building materials), property attributes can be classified into six general categories: site, interior, exterior, quality, location, and market characteristics. The sale price recorded on the deed is the dependent or estimated variable in the regression analysis.[2]

Site Characteristics
Site characteristics are generally represented by two variables: square footage of the site (LOT) and the number of covered or enclosed parking spaces (PARKING). (For a list of the property attributes maintained for Kentlands, see Figure 6-1.) In some data sets, a binary variable is used to represent unusually small lots. LOGLOT is the log transformation of lot size. For several of the communities, the additional value of a square foot of lot diminishes with size. By transforming the lot size variable, each additional square foot of land is not quite as valuable as the prior square foot of land.

Interior Characteristics
Several attributes are included to measure the interior characteristics of each home. AREA is the square footage of interior living area, excluding the basement. A separate binary variable, BASEMENT, is used to identify whether a housing unit has a basement.[3] The BATH variable corresponds to the number of bathrooms in the house, with half bathrooms counted as one-half. Full bathrooms generally have a sink, a toilet, and a bathtub, while a half bath has only a sink and a toilet. FIREPLACE is the number of fireplaces in the house. For some communities, a binary variable representing the floor materials is also included.

Exterior Characteristics
Exterior characteristics generally are described by several groups of binary variables representing roofing material, roof type, exterior facade, number of stories, and type of structure. For example, WSHINGLE and METAL are binary variables that identify

Figure 6-1
Housing Attributes for Kentlands

Attribute	Description
Dependent Variables	
PRICE	Sale price recorded on the deed
LOGPRICE	Natural logarithm of sale price
Site Characteristics	
LOT	Square footage of site
LOGLOT	Natural logarithm of lot size
PARKING	Number of covered or enclosed parking spaces
Interior Characteristics	
AREA	Square footage of interior living area, excluding basement
BATH	Number of bathrooms (bathrooms with only a sink and a toilet are counted as one-half)
BASEMENT	Binary variable 1 if the house has a basement, otherwise 0
FIREPLACE	Number of fireplaces
Exterior Characteristics	
WSHINGLE[a]	Binary variable 1 if the house has a wood shingle roof, otherwise 0
ALUMINUM[b]	Binary variable 1 if the house has an aluminum/vinyl exterior, otherwise 0
BRICK[b]	Binary variable 1 if the house has a brick exterior, otherwise 0
STORY1[c]	Binary variable 1 if number of stories is 1, otherwise 0
STORY3[c]	Binary variable 1 if number of stories is 3, otherwise 0
SPLITFOYER[c]	Binary variable 1 if the house has a split foyer, otherwise 0
TOWNHOME	Binary variable 1 if the property is a townhouse, 0 if it is detached
Quality Characteristics	
GRADE3[d]	Binary variable 1 if the construction quality is grade 3, otherwise 0
GRADE5[d]	Binary variable 1 if the construction quality is grade 5, otherwise 0
GRADE6[d]	Binary variable 1 if the construction quality is grade 6, otherwise 0
AGE	Property age in years
AGESQUARE	Age squared
Location Characteristics	
CENSUS TRACT[e]	Various binary variables
Market Characteristics	
YEAR95[f]	Binary variable 1 if the transaction occurred in 1995, otherwise 0
YEAR96[f]	Binary variable 1 if the transaction occurred in 1996, otherwise 0
YEAR97[f]	Binary variable 1 if the transaction occurred in 1997, otherwise 0
KENTLANDS	Binary variable 1 if the house is in Kentlands, otherwise 0

[a] The reference variable is composite shingle.
[b] The reference variable is wood.
[c] The reference variable is two stories.
[d] The reference variable for quality indicators is grade 4. The quality of construction materials is defined by the Maryland State Department of Assessment and Taxation (MSDAT) in a scale from 1 to 9. Grades 3 to 6 represent "fair," "average," "good," and "very good," respectively. A detailed definition of each category is available in the *Maryland Assessment CAMA System Manual* (1996) by MSDAT.
[e] Nine location binary variables are used to represent census tracts in the zip code 20878: 7006.01, 7006.04, 7006.05, 7006.06, 7006.07, 7007.06, 7008.01, 7008.05, and 7008.06. The reference variable is 7008.06.
[f] The reference year is 1994.

properties with cedar-shingled and metal roofs, different from composite-roofed homes, which is the reference variable.[4] For Harbor Town and Southern Village, the type of roof structure is also included. Exterior building materials vary by community. The most common exterior building material or building structure is the reference variable. Similarly, different types of housing structures are identified with binary variables for single-story *(STORY1)*, three-story *(STORY3)*, and *SPLITFOYER* homes, with two-story homes the reference variable. Properties in Kentlands include both single-family detached homes and townhouses.[5] Because the cost and quality of construction may differ between detached and attached housing, a binary variable (where *TOWNHOME* equals 1) is included to control for the price differential.

Quality Characteristics

To properly measure the impact of the new urbanism on housing value, it is essential to isolate the effects of community planning from other housing characteristics, especially housing quality. The interior and exterior variables may partially reflect the quality of a property; however, additional variables are necessary to explicitly capture the quality differentials among housing units. Three variables are employed to reflect the physical quality and obsolescence of every sale transaction.

Overall construction quality of each property was collected from each municipality. Each analysis includes one or more quality variables *(GRADE)*. In some instances, quality was represented by a group of binary variables representing different quality grades (i.e., from a grade of 4 to a grade of 8). In other communities, the grade variable was included as a scalar variable (i.e., a single variable with a scale of quality ratings). Another proxy for quality is property age. The *AGE* variable is the age of the property in years. A second age variable was included in all of the analyses that squares the age variable. The inclusion of two age variables allows for a nonlinear relationship between property value and age. The *AGESQUARE* variable permits the value of a property to diminish as it becomes older but then to reach a point where property age may no longer reduce a property's value and may actually be a benefit.

Location Characteristics

Location is also important in determining the value of a house. For example, consumers' housing decisions may be influenced by differences in tax rates, quality of school districts, and other neighborhood characteristics such as noise, air pollution, and crime. With the exception of Southern Village and Celebration, all the new urbanist developments and comparable developments are in the same school and tax district. Southern Village, which is located outside the city of

Chapel Hill's boundary but adjacent to the city, uses comparables in the city; it will eventually be annexed by the city. Additionally, the tax rate is 0.355 percent less than for the city of Chapel Hill. Celebration has a series of additional taxes that are not applied to the surrounding community. This tax rate differential is discussed later in the chapter.

A group of binary variables that represents the census tracts in the studied area is used to capture locational differences. The Mud Island *(MUDISLAND)* variable for Harbor Town is included to reveal the differential in price between living on Mud Island and living off the island.

Market Characteristics

Also included in the regression analysis are binary variables representing the time of the sales transaction. These variables are expected to reflect the changing housing market over the period of the study, 1994 to 1997. For Harbor Town and Laguna West, a variable for gated communities *(GATED)* is also included, where properties in gated communities maintain a value of 1, those not in such communities, a value of 0.

Finally, and most important, this study includes a binary variable for new urbanist developments. This variable maintains a value of 1 if the property is located in a new urbanist community and 0 otherwise. The coefficient of this binary variable is the primary focus of the study. The price differential between houses in new urbanist communities and in conventional subdivisions is measured with this coefficient.

Unusual Sales Transactions

To ensure that the data on property sales reflect the behavior of a vast majority of market participants, unusual sales transactions were systematically eliminated based on a ratio of sale price to assessed value. The sale price of a house may deviate from its assessed value to a certain extent, but the sale price of the property is unlikely to be substantially higher or lower than the assessed value. Therefore, transactions that have a sale price that is 60 percent greater than the assessed value or that is less than 60 percent of the assessed value were deleted from the data set. Removal of these outlying observations prevents coding errors, non-arms-length transactions, or a property with unique characteristics from unduly influencing the pricing model.

Another criterion for removing extreme observations was based on the independent variables. Properties whose lot is greater than two acres, with more than five bathrooms, or older than 80 years were excluded to maintain a homogeneous pool of transactions. By comparison, the average transaction for a new urbanist property involved a 7,410-square-foot lot, 2.62 bathrooms, and a dwelling 1.40 years old. Similarly, the average for all sales transactions, including both new urbanist and conventional properties, was a property with a 9,190-square-foot lot and 2.39 bathrooms that was 9.43 years old.

While removing observations from a data set generally returns better regression results, it is necessary not to bias the entire data set in the process. For the Kentlands, Laguna West, Southern Village, Celebration, and Northwest Landing data sets, 4 to 5 percent of the transactions were removed using the parsing techniques discussed earlier. Significantly more observations were eliminated for Harbor Town, however—fully 47.5 percent of the total observations, for a variety of reasons. Of the 1,322 total observations, 319 (24 percent) were removed because the sale price–to–assessed value ratio was either greater than 1.6 or less than 0.6. Another 140 (11 percent) of the observations were eliminated because the properties were older than 80 years of age. Eighteen properties (slightly over 1 percent) were removed for having five or more bathrooms.

Additional outliers were also eliminated from the Harbor Town data set and not the other communities. One property was eliminated because it had a quality rating of more than ten, while nine transactions were removed because the quality rating was less than four. These ten transactions were eliminated because the properties are not comparable to Harbor Town, where over 75 percent of the properties maintain a quality rating of eight or higher and none have a quality rating of less than seven. In addition, two cutoffs were used to remove properties with inordinately low assessed value. If the assessed value of the land was less than $1.00 per square foot or the improvements were assessed at less than $25.00 per square foot, the transaction was removed. Although this cutoff is arbitrary, the average assessed value of land for transactions in Harbor Town was $48.00 per square foot, and improvements on average were valued at $89.00 per square foot.

One possible reason for the large number of unusual observations for Harbor Town is that the comparable area for Harbor Town includes a mature community containing a wide variety of type and quality of housing units. A second possible reason is that the data were obtained directly from the Shelby County Assessor's Office and may not have been thoroughly checked.

The combined and cleaned data set includes information on four different new urbanist communities (not including Northwest Landing and Celebration) with a total of 5,833 sales transactions. Transactions in the new urbanist communities accounted for 664 observations, the remaining 5,169 for comparable properties.

Single-Family Housing Attributes By Community

Each new urbanist community used in the analysis is discussed individually in a similar format to ensure comparability between single-family sales in the new urbanist communities and those in the surrounding market area. Two tables are included in each discussion: a description of housing attributes and summary statistics (averages and ranges of observed variables). A final section discusses the combined data set.

Kentlands

The Kentlands data set includes sales of single-family residences in the city of Gaithersburg and in Montgomery County, Maryland, for 1994 to 1997. Observations were drawn from the zip code 20878. The average sale price for the four-year period was $238,920, ranging from $62,070 to $675,000 (see Figure 6-1 on page 43 and Figure 6-2 below). Of the 2,392 property sales, 291 were in Kentlands and 2,101 were of comparable properties surrounding Kentlands. The average sale prices for a property in Kentlands and in the areas surrounding Kentlands were $294,280 and $231,260, respectively.

To explain the variation in home prices, a total of 32 independent variables was

Figure 6-2
Summary Statistics for Kentlands

Attribute	All Sales (n = 2,392)				Kentlands (n = 291)		Surrounding Area (n = 2,101)	
	Mean	Standard Deviation	Minimum	Maximum	Mean	Standard Deviation	Mean	Standard Deviation
Dependent Variables								
PRICE (000)	238.92	89.23	62.07	675.00	294.28	77.66	231.26	88.03
LOGPRICE	12.31	.39	11.04	13.42	12.56	.25	12.28	.39
Site Characteristics								
LOT (000)	10.33	12.03	.97	87.12	4.03	2.35	11.20	12.56
PARKING	1.47	.53	.00	3.00	1.82	.43	1.42	.53
Interior Characteristics								
AREA (000)	2.12	.78	.92	4.87	2.18	.67	2.12	.79
BATH	2.70	.60	1.00	5.00	2.99	.58	2.66	.59
BASEMENT	.85	.36	.00	1.00	.72	.45	.86	.34
FIREPLACE	.87	.56	.00	3.00	.80	.56	.88	.56
Exterior Characteristics								
WSHINGLE	.19	.39	.00	1.00	.97	.18	.08	.27
ALUMINUM	.27	.45	.00	1.00	.14	.34	.29	.45
BRICK	.11	.31	.00	1.00	.15	.36	.11	.31
STORY1	.05	.22	.00	1.00	.00	.06	.06	.23
STORY3	.02	.18	.00	1.00	.01	.10	.02	.15
SPLITFOYER	.02	.13	.00	1.00	.00	.00	.02	.14
TOWNHOME	.33	.47	.00	1.00	.41	.49	.32	.47
Quality Characteristics								
GRADE3	.03	.18	.00	1.00	.04	.18	.00	.00
GRADE5	.35	.48	.00	1.00	.29	.45	.80	.39
GRADE6	.03	.16	.00	1.00	.01	.11	.13	.33
AGE	10.05	8.21	.00	72.00	.79	1.43	11.33	7.94
Market Characteristics								
YEAR95	.29	.45	.00	1.00	.23	.42	.29	.46
YEAR96	.23	.42	.00	1.00	.12	.33	.24	.43
YEAR97	.15	.35	.00	1.00	.07	.25	.16	.36
KENTLANDS	.12	.33	.00	1.00	—	—	—	—

employed. Site characteristics were represented by the natural log of lot size and the number of covered or enclosed parking stalls on the site. The average lot size in Kentlands is much smaller than the surrounding area (4,030 versus 11,200 square feet, respectively).[6] Based on the literature, the differential in lot sizes is expected. Kentlands properties have slightly more covered parking (garage space) than the surrounding area.

Four variables were used to compare the interior space of the housing units: square feet of living area, number of bathrooms, existence of a basement, and number of fireplaces. On average, both the Kentlands and comparable properties maintained similar interior characteristics.

Exterior characteristics used several groups of binary variables to account for property differentials. One significant difference between Kentlands and the surrounding developments is that most all Kentlands homes have wood-shingled roofs (97 percent), while only 8 percent of the comparable units do. The remaining exterior characteristics are largely the same.

The quality of housing construction for the area is designated by the Maryland State Department of Assessment and Taxation. The range for single-family housing is from one (low) to nine (high), represented in the analysis by a series of *GRADE* binary variables, where grade four is the reference variable. The average grade in the data set is 4.37, with a range of three to six. Separate binary variables were employed instead of a single scalar variable to account for the possibility of a nonlinear relationship between grade and unit price. The average age of housing units in Kentlands is approximately one year and in the surrounding community is about 11 years, which is controlled for by using two variables, *AGE* and *AGESQUARE.*

Location and time variables were also used in the regression models. The location of a property was represented by a group of census tract variables. While census tracts do not always follow community lines, they control for the possibility of locational price differentials across the 20878 zip code. To account for the possibility of property appreciation (depreciation) over the period of analysis, three binary variables were used, each with roughly the same number of transactions year over year and across the new urbanist development and the comparables. Twelve percent of all single-family sales transactions occurred in Kentlands.

Harbor Town

Harbor Town was the only market in the study where FARES data were not available; therefore, the entire data set was acquired from the Shelby County, Tennessee, Assessor's Office. Observations were drawn from sales of single-family detached houses in the neighborhood code 00701 from 1994 to 1997. This area includes all of Mud Island and a portion of downtown Memphis. The average sale price for the four-year period was $104,900, ranging from $25,000 to $385,370 (see Figures 6-3 and 6-4). Of the 694 property sales, 79 were in Harbor Town and 615 in comparable properties surrounding Harbor Town.

The average sale prices for a property in Harbor Town and in the areas surrounding Harbor Town were $204,340 and $92,120, respectively. This $112,220 average differential in sale price calls into question the comparability of the property sales for Harbor Town and the surrounding market area. There appear to be three primary reasons for this differential. First, many of the comparable properties located east of Wolf River are older. Second, amenities for properties on Mud Island may be different from those east of the river. Third, the difference may be attributable to Harbor Town's new urbanist design.

Because of the large differential in sale prices, Harbor Town was compared with other properties built on Mud Island after 1980 to see whether comparables existed for Harbor Town. Comparing Harbor Town

Figure 6-3
Housing Attributes for Harbor Town

Attribute	Description
Dependent Variables	
PRICE	Sale price recorded on the deed
LOGPRICE	Natural logarithm of sale price
Site Characteristics	
LOT	Square footage of site
LOGLOT	Natural logarithm of lot size
PARKING	Number of covered or enclosed parking spaces
Interior Characteristics	
AREA	Square footage of interior living area, excluding basement
BATH	Number of bathrooms (bathrooms with only a sink and a toilet are counted as one-half)
BASEMENT	Binary variable 1 if the house has a basement, otherwise 0
FIREPLACE	Number of fireplaces
Exterior Characteristics	
FRAME[a]	Binary variable 1 if the house has a frame exterior, otherwise 0
STUCCO[a]	Binary variable 1 if the house has a stucco exterior, otherwise 0
VINYL[a]	Binary variable 1 if the house has a vinyl exterior, otherwise 0
STONE[a]	Binary variable 1 if the house has a stone exterior, otherwise 0
BRICKFRAME[a]	Binary variable 1 if the house has a brick/frame exterior, otherwise 0
HIP[b]	Binary variable 1 if the house has a hip roof, otherwise 0
STORY2[c]	Binary variable 1 if number of stories is 2, otherwise 0
STORY3[c]	Binary variable 1 if number of stories is 3, otherwise 0
Quality Characteristics	
GRADE[d]	Quality of construction materials
AGE	Property age in years
AGESQUARE	Age squared
Location Characteristics	
MUDISLAND	Binary variable 1 if the property is located on Mud Island, otherwise 0
Market Characteristics	
YEAR95[e]	Binary variable 1 if the transaction occurred in 1995, otherwise 0
YEAR96[e]	Binary variable 1 if the transaction occurred in 1996, otherwise 0
YEAR97[e]	Binary variable 1 if the transaction occurred in 1997, otherwise 0
GATED	Binary variable 1 if the property is in a gated community, otherwise 0
HARBORTOWN	Binary variable 1 if the house is in Harbor Town, otherwise 0

[a] The reference variable is brick veneer.
[b] The reference variable is a gable roof.
[c] The reference variable is one story.
[d] The reference variable is grade 6. In this study, quality indicators were rescaled as 2 (lowest quality) to 14 (highest quality), with 6 representing "average." The quality of property is assigned by the Shelby County Assessor's Office. The quality is defined in a scale of 10 to 70 at intervals of 5.
[e] The reference year is 1994.

with Mud Island properties built after 1980 controls for both the locational effect of Mud Island and the effect of age. Across all descriptive statistics, the difference between Harbor Town and conventional developments built after 1980 on Mud Island was much more muted than for other properties in the 00701 neighborhood. (All sales of properties on Mud Island built since 1980 were of properties located in gated communities.) Specifically, the average sale prices

for homes built after 1980 in Harbor Town and on the rest of Mud Island were $204,340 and $225,363, respectively. For this subset of observations, the comparables maintained a $21,023 higher average sale price than in Harbor Town.

To explain the variation in home prices, a total of 28 independent variables was employed. Site characteristics were represented by the natural log of lot size and the number of parking spaces on the site. The

Figure 6-4
Summary Statistics for Harbor Town

Attribute	All Sales (n = 694)				Harbor Town (n = 79)		Surrounding Area (n = 615)	
	Mean	Standard Deviation	Minimum	Maximum	Mean	Standard Deviation	Mean	Standard Deviation
Dependent Variables								
PRICE (000)	104.90	71.39	25.00	385.37	204.34	73.41	92.12	60.26
LOGPRICE	11.38	.57	10.12	12.86	12.17	.33	11.28	.52
Site Characteristics								
LOT (000)	5.27	2.50	1.03	21.10	4.23	1.56	5.41	2.56
PARKING	.71	.85	.00	3.00	1.65	.77	.59	.80
Interior Characteristics								
AREA (000)	1.60	.65	.67	5.13	2.31	.66	1.51	.59
BATH	1.65	.73	1.00	4.50	2.63	.46	1.52	.66
BASEMENT	.64	.48	.00	1.00	.48	.50	.66	.47
FIREPLACE	.78	.88	.00	3.00	.99	.65	.75	.90
Exterior Characteristics								
FRAME	.31	.46	.00	1.00	.85	.36	.24	.43
STUCCO	.03	.17	.00	1.00	.01	.11	.03	.17
VINYL	.08	.27	.00	1.00	.00	.00	.09	.29
STONE	.01	.12	.00	1.00	.00	.00	.02	.13
BRICKFRAME	.02	.15	.00	1.00	.02	.15	.02	.14
HIP	.16	.37	.00	1.00	.14	.34	.16	.37
STORY2	.28	.45	.00	1.00	.80	.40	.21	.41
STORY3	.04	.19	.00	1.00	.20	.40	.02	.13
Quality Characteristics								
GRADE	6.25	1.19	4.00	10.00	8.00	.77	7.00	10.00
AGE	39.34	26.39	.00	80.00	2.53	2.25	44.07	24.26
Location Characteristic								
MUDISLAND	.18	.39	.00	1.00	1.00	.00	.08	.27
Market Characteristics								
YEAR95	.24	.43	.00	1.00	.15	.36	.25	.43
YEAR96	.27	.44	.00	1.00	.30	.46	.27	.44
YEAR97	.29	.45	.00	1.00	.28	.45	.29	.46
GATED	.02	.12	.00	1.00	.00	.00	.02	.13
HARBORTOWN	.11	.32	.00	1.00	—	—	—	—

average lot in Harbor Town is smaller than the surrounding area, at 4,230 and 5,410 square feet, respectively. Transactions for Harbor Town also have approximately one more covered parking space than the surrounding area.

Four variables were used to compare the interior space of housing units: square feet of living area, number of bathrooms, existence of a basement, and number of fireplaces. On average, Harbor Town units are 800 square feet larger than the comparables, but when Harbor Town units are compared with the comparables on Mud Island, Harbor Town units are on average only 57 square feet larger. Harbor Town housing units have approximately one more bathroom than the comparables but have the same number of bathrooms as the Mud Island comparables. The variables for basement and fireplace in the new urbanist community generally resemble those outside the community.

Two significant differences in exterior characteristics are apparent between Harbor Town and the surrounding developments.

First, 85 percent of Harbor Town houses have a wood exterior, while only 24 percent of housing units in the surrounding area do. Second, Harbor Town homes are all two- and three-story units, while only 23 percent in the surrounding area are. Once again, when Harbor Town was compared with Mud Island only, differences in exterior characteristics were much more muted. The remaining exterior characteristics were largely the same.

The Shelby County Assessor's Office designates the quality of housing construction in the county. The quality for single-family housing ranges from one (low) to 12 (high). The data set has an average quality rating of 6.22. Construction quality is represented by a series of binary variables for grade, where grade six is the reference variable. The average age of housing units in Harbor Town is approximately three years and in the surrounding community about 44 years, with the comparables on Mud Island built after 1980 maintaining an average age of 4.1. Age was controlled for in the regression analysis using two variables, *AGE* and *AGESQUARE*.

Location and time variables were also used in the regression models. Properties located on Mud Island may be affected by factors not related to properties off the island, such as the threat of a flood, accessibility to amenities, and traffic. A single location variable was used to identify the properties located on Mud Island to account for these differences. Eighteen percent of the transactions occurred on Mud Island.

To account for changing single-family prices over the period 1994 to 1997, three binary variables were employed, each with roughly the same number of transactions year over year and across the new urbanist community and the comparables. Additionally, a gated community is located on Mud Island that is not part of Harbor Town. To account for the possibility of a price differential between gated and nongated communities, the binary variable *GATED* was

included. Eleven percent of all single-family sales occurred in Harbor Town.

Laguna West

Laguna West's data set includes sales of single-family residences in the zip code 95758 for 1994 to 1997. The zip code is located in Elk Grove, California, approximately 12 miles south of downtown Sacramento. The average sale price for the four-year analysis period was $143,690, ranging from $57,500 to $317,000 (see Figures 6-5 and 6-6). Of the 3,303 property sales, 326 were in Laguna West and 2,977 were in comparable properties surrounding Laguna West. The average sale prices for a property in Laguna West and in the areas surrounding Laguna West were $166,110 and $141,230, respectively.

Twenty independent variables were used to explain the variation in home prices. Site characteristics were represented by the natural log of lot size and the number of covered or enclosed parking stalls on the site. The average size of lots and number of parking spaces in Laguna West closely resembled the surrounding area.

Four variables were used to compare the interior space of the housing units: square feet of living area, number of bathrooms, existence of a basement, and number of fireplaces. On average, both Laguna West and the comparable properties maintained similar interior characteristics. None of the housing units in the data set had a basement, and all units had a fireplace. Because all properties had the same attributes for basement and fireplace, the regression model could not determine a value differential as such, so neither attribute is included in the regression model.

Exterior characteristics used four groups of binary variables: roof material, exterior wall material, existence of a swimming pool, and number of stories. On average, exterior characteristics of units sold in Laguna West closely re-

Figure 6-5

Housing Attributes for Laguna West

Attribute	Description
Dependent Variables	
PRICE	Sale price recorded on the deed
LOGPRICE	Natural logarithm of sale price
Site Characteristics	
LOT	Square footage of site
LOGLOT	Natural logarithm of lot size
PARKING	Number of covered or enclosed parking spaces
Interior Characteristics	
AREA	Square footage of interior living area, excluding basement
BATH	Number of bathrooms (bathrooms with only a sink and a toilet are counted as one-half)
BASEMENT	Binary variable 1 if the house has a basement, otherwise 0
FIREPLACE	Number of fireplaces
Exterior Characteristics	
COMPOSITE[a]	Binary variable 1 if the house has a composite shingle roof, otherwise 0
WOOD[b]	Binary variable 1 if the house has a wood siding exterior, otherwise 0
POOL	Binary variable 1 if the property has a pool, otherwise 0
STORY2[c]	Binary variable 1 if number of stories is 2, otherwise 0
Quality Characteristics	
EXCELLENT[d]	Binary variable 1 if quality of the property is excellent, otherwise 0
GOOD[d]	Binary variable 1 if quality of the property is good, otherwise 0
POOR[d]	Binary variable 1 if quality of the property is poor, otherwise 0
AGE	Property age in years
AGESQUARE	Age squared
Location Characteristics	
CENSUS TRACT[e]	Binary variable
Market Characteristics	
YEAR95[f]	Binary variable 1 if the transaction occurred in 1995, otherwise 0
YEAR96[f]	Binary variable 1 if the transaction occurred in 1996, otherwise 0
YEAR97[f]	Binary variable 1 if the transaction occurred in 1997, otherwise 0
GATED	Binary variable 1 if the property is located in a gated community, otherwise 0
LAKEVIEW	Binary variable 1 if the property has a lake view, otherwise 0
LAGUNAWEST	Binary variable 1 if the house is in Laguna West, otherwise 0

[a] The reference variable is wood shake.
[b] The reference variable is stucco.
[c] The reference variable is one story.
[d] The Sacramento County Assessor's Office assigns the quality of construction materials as "poor," "average," "good," and "excellent." The reference variable for quality in the analysis is average.
[e] A binary variable for location was used to separate the census tracts in the zip code.
[f] The reference year is 1994.

sembled those of developments in the surrounding area.

The Sacramento County Assessor's Office designates the quality of housing construction for the county. The quality of single-family housing in the data set is classified as "poor," "average," "good," or "excellent." Each category is represented in the analysis with a binary variable, where "average" is the reference variable, with 86 percent of the observations. The average age of housing units in Laguna West is approximately one year and in the surrounding community is about three years.

To account for the change in single-family sale prices from 1994 to 1997, three binary variables were used, with 1994 being the reference variable. Two binary variables were used to account for housing units in a gated community *(GATED)* and housing

Figure 6-6
Summary Statistics for Laguna West

Attribute	All Sales (n = 3,303)				Laguna West (n = 326)		Surrounding Area (n = 2,977)	
	Mean	Standard Deviation	Minimum	Maximum	Mean	Standard Deviation	Mean	Standard Deviation
Dependent Variables								
PRICE (000)	143.69	32.44	57.50	317.00	166.11	31.66	141.23	31.58
LOGPRICE	11.85	.20	10.96	12.67	12.00	.19	11.84	.20
Site Characteristics								
LOT (000)	6.37	3.08	2.18	56.19	6.56	3.54	6.35	3.02
PARKING	2.22	.42	.00	3.00	2.30	.46	2.21	.42
Interior Characteristics								
AREA (000)	1.67	.42	.83	3.95	1.80	.38	1.66	.42
BATH	2.32	.39	1.00	4.00	2.46	.45	2.31	.38
BASEMENT	.00	.00	.00	0.00	0.00	.00	0.00	.00
FIREPLACE	1.00	.00	1.00	1.00	1.00	.00	1.00	.00
Exterior Characteristics								
COMPOSITE	.09	.28	.00	1.00	.05	.22	.05	.22
WOOD	.05	.22	.00	1.00	.00	.06	.06	.23
POOL	.05	.23	.00	1.00	.05	.22	.05	.23
STORY2	.47	.50	.00	1.00	.56	.50	.46	.50
Quality Characteristics								
EXCELLENT	.00	.06	.00	1.00	.03	.16	.00	.04
GOOD	.13	.34	.00	1.00	.37	.48	.11	.31
POOR	.01	.07	.00	1.00	.00	.06	.01	.07
AGE	2.47	3.45	.00	58.00	.65	1.16	2.67	3.57
Market Characteristics								
YEAR95	.24	.42	.00	1.00	.25	.43	.24	.43
YEAR96	.29	.45	.00	1.00	.33	.47	.29	.45
YEAR97	.17	.37	.00	1.00	.14	.35	.17	.38
GATED	.01	.11	.00	1.00	.00	.00	.01	.11
LAKEVIEW	.04	.20	.00	1.00	.29	.45	.01	.11
LAGUNAWEST	.10	.30	.00	1.00	—	—	—	—

units with a lake view *(LAKEVIEW)*. Ten percent of all single-family sales occurred in Laguna West.

Southern Village

Southern Village's data set includes sales of single-family residences in the township of Chapel Hill, Orange County, North Carolina, for 1994 to 1997.[7] The average sale price for the four-year analysis period was $221,800, ranging from $69,500 to $425,000 (see Figures 6-7 and 6-8). Of the 503 property sales, 82 occurred in Southern Village, the remaining 421 in comparable properties near Southern Village. The average sale prices for properties in Southern

Village and in the comparable areas were $240,410 and $217,180, respectively.

A total of 32 independent variables was used to explain the variation in home prices. Site characteristics include lot size and the number of covered or enclosed parking stalls. The average lot in Southern Village is slightly larger than the average lot in the comparable area, 17,450 versus 15,510 square feet, respectively. Properties sold in Southern Village had slightly more covered parking.

Five variables were used to compare the interior space of housing units: square feet of living area, square feet of nonliving area, number of bathrooms, existence of a base-

Figure 6-7
Housing Attributes for Southern Village

Attribute	Description
Dependent Variables	
PRICE	Sale price recorded on the deed
LOGPRICE	Natural logarithm of sale price
Site Characteristics	
LOT	Square footage of site
SMALL	Binary variable 1 if lot is less than one-sixth of an acre, otherwise 0
PARKING	Number of covered or enclosed parking spaces
Interior Characteristics	
AREA	Square footage of interior living area, excluding basement
ADDITION	Square footage of additional (nonliving) area
BATH	Number of bathrooms (bathrooms with only a sink and a toilet are counted as one-half)
BASEMENT	Binary variable 1 if the house has a basement, otherwise 0
FIREPLACE	Number of fireplaces
HARDWOOD[a]	Binary variable 1 if the house has hardwood floors, otherwise 0
TILE[a]	Binary variable 1 if the house has tile floors, otherwise 0
Exterior Characteristics	
METAL[b]	Binary variable 1 if the house has a metal roof, otherwise 0
HIP[c]	Binary variable 1 if the house has a hip roof, otherwise 0
SLAB[d]	Binary variable 1 if the foundation is slab, otherwise 0
STORY1[e]	Binary variable 1 if number of stories is 1, otherwise 0
Quality Characteristics	
GRADE[f]	Quality of construction materials
AGE	Property age in years
AGESQUARE	Age squared
Location Characteristics	
CENSUS TRACT[g]	Various binary variables
Market Characteristics	
YEAR95[h]	Binary variable 1 if the transaction occurred in 1995, otherwise 0
YEAR96[h]	Binary variable 1 if the transaction occurred in 1996, otherwise 0
YEAR97[h]	Binary variable 1 if the transaction occurred in 1997, otherwise 0
SOUTHERN	Binary variable 1 if the house is in Southern Village, otherwise 0

[a] The reference variable is carpet.
[b] The reference variable is composite shingle.
[c] The reference variable is gable.
[d] The reference variable is masonry.
[e] The reference variable is two stories.
[f] Orange County, North Carolina, defines the quality of construction materials. The quality indicator ranges from 0 (lowest) to 2.5 (highest) at intervals of 0.05.
[g] A group of 11 location binary variables represents the census tracts in the township of Chapel Hill.
[h] The reference year is 1994.

ment, and number of fireplaces. On average, Southern Village and the comparable area maintained very similar interior housing characteristics. Moreover, the exterior attributes of the new urbanist community closely resembled those found in the conventional properties in the area surrounding Southern Village.

The Orange County Tax Office designates the quality of housing construction for Orange County. The quality of single-family housing ranged from 0 (low) to 2.5 (high), at intervals of 0.05.[8] The average grade in the data set was 1.49, ranging from 0.8 to 1.9. The quality of construction was almost the same both inside and outside the new urbanist community, at approximately 1.5. The average age of housing units in Southern Village is approximately two and one-half years, that

Figure 6-8
Summary Statistics for Southern Village

Attribute	All Sales (n = 503)				Southern Village (n = 82)		Surrounding Area (n = 421)	
	Mean	Standard Deviation	Minimum	Maximum	Mean	Standard Deviation	Mean	Standard Deviation
Dependent Variables								
PRICE (000)	221.80	57.72	69.50	425.00	240.41	30.21	217.18	61.21
LOGPRICE	12.27	.29	11.15	12.96	12.38	.12	12.24	.31
Site Characteristics								
LOT (000)	15.85	11.47	1.80	80.37	17.45	.8.63	15.51	11.96
SMALL	.20	.40	.00	1.00	.14	.35	.21	.40
PARKING	1.43	.94	.00	3.00	1.85	.88	1.34	.92
Interior Characteristics								
AREA (000)	1.48	.36	.58	2.80	1.34	.31	1.51	.36
ADDITION	11.30	50.32	.00	384.00	9.24	42.91	12.28	51.77
BATH	2.51	.43	1.50	4.50	2.58	.28	2.49	.45
BASEMENT	.09	.29	.00	1.00	.03	.18	.10	.30
FIREPLACE	.98	.32	.00	3.00	1.01	.11	.97	.35
HARDWOOD	.41	.49	.00	1.00	.60	.49	.37	.48
TILE	.02	.14	.00	1.00	.00	.00	.02	.15
Exterior Characteristics								
METAL	.02	.15	.00	1.00	.00	.00	.03	.16
HIP	.18	.39	.00	1.00	.16	.37	.19	.39
SLAB	.02	.14	.00	1.00	.00	.00	.02	.15
STORY1	.14	.35	.00	1.00	.02	.15	.17	.37
Quality Characteristics								
GRADE	1.49	.15	.80	1.90	1.54	.13	1.48	.15
AGE	6.57	13.78	.00	74.00	2.51	2.52	7.36	13.79
Market Characteristics								
YEAR95	.34	.47	.00	1.00	.32	.47	.34	.47
YEAR96	.35	.48	.00	1.00	.46	.50	.32	.46
YEAR97	.14	.34	.00	1.00	.21	.41	.12	.32
SOUTHERN	.16	.37	.00	1.00	—	—	—	—

of the comparable communities about seven and one-half.

The location of a property was represented by a group of census tract variables. While census tracts do not always follow community lines, they control for the possibility of locational price differentials across the township. To account for the possibility of changing property values over the period of analysis, three binary variables were used, each with roughly the same number of transactions year over year and across the new urbanist development and the comparables. Sixteen percent of all single-family sales transactions occurred in Southern Village.

Northwest Landing

Data for Northwest Landing and its surrounding area came from the city of Du Pont, Washington. Over the three-year period 1995 to 1997 (sales of residential units began in 1995), only 59 sales occurred in the city, 55 in Northwest Landing and four in the historic village. No other residential areas are located close to the city of Du Pont: Fort Lewis, an Army base, is located adjacent to the city, and the nearest residential area is Steilacoom, approximately six miles away. The lack of comparable housing units in the surrounding area made it impossible to reasonably estimate the price differential with a regression model. For this reason, Northwest Landing was removed from the regression analysis.

Celebration

Celebration's data set includes sales of single-family residences in Osceola County, Florida, for 1995 to 1997. Observations were drawn from the zip code 34747. The average sale price for the analysis period was $146,600, ranging from $73,000 to $815,000 (see Figures 6-9 and 6-10). Of the 489 property sales transactions, 89 occurred in Celebration and 400 in properties surrounding Celebration. The average sale prices for a property in Celebration and in the areas surrounding Celebration were $279,510 and $117,030, respectively. Similar to Harbor Town, the large price differential between Celebration and the surrounding area ($162,480) was cause for concern.

Figure 6-9

Housing Attributes for Celebration

Attribute	Description
Dependent Variables	
PRICE	Sale price recorded on the deed
LOGPRICE	Natural logarithm of sale price
Site Characteristics	
LOT	Square footage of site
LOGLOT	Natural logarithm of lot size
Interior Characteristics	
AREA	Square footage of interior living area, excluding basement
BATH	Number of bathrooms (bathrooms with only a sink and a toilet are counted as one-half)
BASEMENT	Binary variable 1 if the house has a basement, otherwise 0
FIREPLACE	Number of fireplaces
PARQUET[a]	Binary variable 1 if the house has parquet floors, otherwise 0
Exterior Characteristics	
SIDING[b]	Binary variable 1 if the house has a single siding exterior, otherwise 0
STUCCO[b]	Binary variable 1 if the house has a stucco exterior, otherwise 0
POOL	Binary variable 1 if the property has a pool, otherwise 0
STORY2[c]	Binary variable 1 if number of stories is 2, otherwise 0
STORY3[c]	Binary variable 1 if number of stories is 3, otherwise 0
Quality Characteristics	
GRADE3[d]	Binary variable 1 if the construction quality is grade 3, otherwise 0
GRADE4[d]	Binary variable 1 if the construction quality is grade 4, otherwise 0
GRADE6[d]	Binary variable 1 if the construction quality is grade 6, otherwise 0
GRADE7[d]	Binary variable 1 if the construction quality is grade 7, otherwise 0
AGE	Property age in years
AGESQUARE	Age squared
Location Characteristics	
TOWNSHIP[e]	Various binary variables
Market Characteristics	
YEAR96[f]	Binary variable 1 if the transaction occurred in 1996, otherwise 0
YEAR97[f]	Binary variable 1 if the transaction occurred in 1997, otherwise 0
GOLF	Binary variable 1 if the property has a golf course view, otherwise 0
CELEBRATION	Binary variable 1 if the house is in Celebration, otherwise 0

[a] The reference variable is carpet.
[b] The reference variable is concrete block.
[c] The reference variable is one story.
[d] The reference variable is grade 5. The Osceola County property appraiser's office defines the quality of construction materials, ranging from 1 (lowest) to 7 (highest).
[e] A group of location binary variables represents the townships in zip code 34747.
[f] The reference year is 1995.

Figure 6-10
Summary Statistics for Celebration

Attribute	All Sales (n = 489)				Celebration (n = 89)		Surrounding Area (n = 400)	
	Mean	Standard Deviation	Minimum	Maximum	Mean	Standard Deviation	Mean	Standard Deviation
Dependent Variables								
PRICE (000)	146.60	82.93	73.00	815.00	279.51	109.46	117.03	30.85
LOGPRICE	11.79	.41	11.19	13.61	12.49	.27	11.63	.24
Site Characteristics								
LOT (000)	7.78	2.50	2.82	19.62	7.32	2.54	7.89	2.49
Interior Characteristics								
AREA (000)	1.87	.56	1.09	5.30	2.66	.72	1.69	.30
BATH	2.24	.51	2.00	5.50	2.88	.83	2.11	.29
PARQUET	.02	.14	.00	1.00	.11	.31	.00	.00
Exterior Characteristics								
SIDING	.15	.35	.00	1.00	.82	.38	.00	.05
STUCCO	.07	.25	.00	1.00	.13	.34	.05	.23
POOL	.32	.46	.00	1.00	.00	.00	.39	.49
STORY2	.12	.21	.00	1.00	.44	.50	.16	.44
STORY3	.01	.11	.00	1.00	.06	.25	.00	.00
Quality Characteristics								
GRADE3	.02	.13	.00	1.00	.00	.00	.02	.14
GRADE4	.72	.44	.00	1.00	.00	.00	.88	.31
GRADE6	.17	.37	.00	1.00	.96	.20	.00	.00
GRADE7	.01	.09	.00	1.00	.04	.20	.00	.00
AGE	2.59	2.86	.00	10.00	.13	.34	3.14	2.88
Market Characteristics								
YEAR96	.47	.50	.00	1.00	.86	.34	.38	.48
YEAR97	.27	.44	.00	1.00	.13	.34	.30	.46
GOLF	.02	.14	.00	1.00	.09	.28	.00	.00
CELEBRATION	.18	.38	.00	1.00	—	—	—	—

A variety of independent variables were used to explain the variation in prices. Site characteristics are represented by natural log of lot size. The average lot in Celebration is slightly smaller than in the surrounding area, 7,320 versus 7,890 square feet, respectively. Differing from the other analyses, no information was available on the number of covered or enclosed parking spaces for the Celebration data set.

Five variables were used to compare the interior space of housing units: square feet of living area, number of bathrooms, existence of a basement, number of fireplaces, and floor materials. Housing units in Celebration are close to 1,000 square feet larger than units in the developments surrounding Celebration. Similarly, sales transactions in Celebration show that the number of bathrooms was 2.88, somewhat higher than in conventional communities, at 2.11 bathrooms per housing unit. The transaction data reveal that no properties in the area have basements or fireplaces.

Similar to interior characteristics, exterior attributes of housing in Celebration were quite different from the conventional properties. In Celebration, 82 percent of the housing units are covered with siding, compared with none in the surrounding community. The existence of a pool also reveals significant differences between the new urbanist and conventional properties. No homes sold in Celebration had a pool, while 39 percent outside Celebration did. One other notable difference between the two is that 50 percent of Celebration's housing units have only one story, while 84 percent of conventional units have only one story.

The Osceola County property appraiser designates the quality of housing construction. The quality ranges from 1 (low) to 7 (high) and is represented by a series of binary variables. All of the housing units in Celebration maintained a grade of six or higher, while 90 percent of the housing units in the surrounding area had a grade of four or less, and none were higher than five. The discrepancy in quality between Celebration and surrounding areas may cause serious problems in the regression analysis.

Further highlighting the differences between Celebration and the communities surrounding it, Celebration has a variety of additional taxes and municipal charges that do not exist for the surrounding communities. While a regression analysis using these data reveals a significant and large premium for the new urbanist binary variable, the authors believe that these results could be attributed to a variety of factors other than the new urbanism. As stated earlier, the best data set to measure the price differential between new urbanist housing and conventional housing is to have all factors other than the new urbanism be the same or as similar as possible. The vast differences between the units in Celebration and the surrounding areas make the results of a hedonic model susceptible to a variety of problems, making it an unacceptable candidate for the analysis.

Combined Data Set

The combined data set includes sales of single-family residences for municipalities in Maryland, Tennessee, California, and North Carolina for 1994 to 1997. The average sale price for the four analyses was $182,410, ranging from $25,000 to $675,000 (see Figures 6-11 and 6-12). Of the 5,833 total property sales,[9] 664 were in new urbanist developments and 5,169 in comparable properties surrounding the new urbanist developments. The average sale prices for a property in one of the new urbanist developments and in the surrounding areas were $224,220 and $177,030, respectively.

A total of 18 independent variables was used to explain the variation in home prices. Site characteristics were represented by lot size and the number of covered or enclosed parking stalls on the site. The average lot in the new urbanist properties was smaller than that in the surrounding area, 7,410 versus 9,420 square feet, respectively. The new urbanist properties had slightly more parking than the surrounding areas.

Four variables were used to compare the interior space of housing units: square feet of living area, number of bathrooms, existence of a basement, and number of fireplaces. Overall, the new urbanist properties and the comparable properties maintained remarkably similar interior characteristics.

The only exterior characteristic that was the same across all data sets was the number of stories. The number of stories for the new urbanist properties was similar to conventional housing, except that 4 percent of the new urbanist units were three story, while less than 1 percent were in the surrounding communities.

Housing quality is based on two attributes, quality of construction and age. Quality of construction as defined by each municipal government varies in both the definition of quality and in how quality is scaled. For instance, Orange County designates a range of 0 (low) to 2.5 (high) with intervals of 0.05, while Shelby County designates a range of 10 (low) to 70 (high) with intervals of 5. To include a scalar that is similar for all the combined sales transactions, the quality variable was transformed to fit a range between 0 and 1. In rescaling the data for quality, the authors reconstructed a relevant quality range based on the construction quality

Figure 6-11

Housing Attributes for Combined Data Set

Attribute	Description
Dependent Variables	
PRICE	Sale price recorded on the deed
LOGPRICE	Natural logarithm of sale price
Site Characteristics	
LOT	Square footage of site
LOGLOT	Natural logarithm of lot size
PARKING	Number of covered or enclosed parking spaces
Interior Characteristics	
AREA	Square footage of interior living area, excluding basement
BATH	Number of bathrooms (bathrooms with only a sink and a toilet are counted as one-half)
BASEMENT	Binary variable 1 if the house has a basement, otherwise 0
FIREPLACE	Number of fireplaces
Exterior Characteristics	
STORY1[a]	Binary variable 1 if number of stories is 1, otherwise 0
STORY3[a]	Binary variable 1 if number of stories is 3, otherwise 0
Quality Characteristics	
GRADE[b]	Quality of construction materials
AGE	Property age in years
AGESQUARE	Age squared
Location Characteristics	
MD[c]	Binary variable 1 if the property is located in Maryland, otherwise 0
TN[c]	Binary variable 1 if the property is located in Tennessee, otherwise 0
NC[c]	Binary variable 1 if the property is located in North Carolina, otherwise 0
Market Characteristics	
YEAR95[d]	Binary variable 1 if the transaction occurred in 1995, otherwise 0
YEAR96[d]	Binary variable 1 if the transaction occurred in 1996, otherwise 0
YEAR97[d]	Binary variable 1 if the transaction occurred in 1997, otherwise 0
NU	Binary variable 1 if the house is in one of the new urbanist developments (traditional neighborhood developments), otherwise 0

[a] The reference variable is two stories.
[b] The quality indicator was rescaled to the range of 0 to 1, with 0.5 average.
[c] The location variables represent the geographical location of a property. The reference variable is California.
[d] The reference variable is 1994.

range in each data set. The average rescaled quality *(GRADE)* for the new urbanist developments was 0.62 and for the conventional developments was 0.55. The other housing quality variable was the age of a property. The average age of new urbanist housing units was approximately one and one-half years, that of the surrounding community about ten and one-half years.

The location of a property was represented by a group of variables using the state where the new urbanist communities are located, with the reference variable being the Laguna West development in California.

To account for the possibility of differential property sales over the period 1994 to 1997, three binary variables were employed, each with roughly the same number of transactions year over year and across the new urbanist development and the comparables. Eleven percent of all single-family sales occurred in new urbanist developments.

In summary, two of the communities considered for regression analysis, Northwest Landing and Celebration, significant differences between the new urbanist and conventional properties prevented further analysis. In both cases, the area surround-

Figure 6-12
Summary Statistics for Combined Data Set

Attribute	All Sales (n = 5,833)				New Urbanist Development (n = 664)		Surrounding Area (n = 5,169)	
	Mean	Standard Deviation	Minimum	Maximum	Mean	Standard Deviation	Mean	Standard Deviation
Dependent Variables								
PRICE (000)	182.41	85.43	25.00	675.00	224.22	87.14	177.03	83.74
LOGPRICE	12.01	.47	10.13	13.42	12.25	.36	11.98	.47
Site Characteristics								
LOT (000)	9.19	8.89	1.03	87.12	7.41	5.79	9.42	9.18
PARKING	1.80	.76	.00	3.00	2.04	.63	1.77	.77
Interior Characteristics								
AREA (000)	1.86	.65	.58	5.13	1.99	.64	1.84	.65
BATH	2.39	.60	1.00	5.00	2.62	.52	2.35	.60
BASEMENT	.32	.47	.00	1.00	.25	.43	.32	.47
FIREPLACE	.98	.42	.00	3.00	1.00	.33	.98	.43
Exterior Characteristics								
STORY1	.38	.49	.00	1.00	.22	.41	.40	.49
STORY3	.01	.08	.00	1.00	.04	.20	.00	.05
Quality Characteristics								
GRADE	.55	.11	.20	1.00	.62	.14	.55	.10
AGE	9.43	15.98	.00	80.00	1.40	4.24	10.47	16.63
Location Characteristics								
MD	.27	.45	.00	1.00	.25	.44	.27	.45
TN	.12	.32	.00	1.00	.11	.32	.12	.32
CA	.52	.50	.00	1.00	.49	.50	.52	.50
NC	.09	.28	.00	1.00	.13	.34	.08	.27
Market Characteristics								
YEAR95	.25	.43	.00	1.00	.24	.43	.25	.44
YEAR96	.26	.44	.00	1.00	.28	.45	.26	.44
YEAR97	.20	.40	.00	1.00	.16	.37	.20	.40
NU	.11	.32	.00	1.00	—	—	—	—

ing the new urbanist community does not include a sufficient number of comparable housing units. Data for the remaining four communities, Kentlands, Harbor Town, Laguna West, and Southern Village, as well as the four communities combined, were further analyzed using regression models.

Notes

1. One of the limitations of regression analysis is the way missing data fields are handled. If data are missing from any of the data fields (e.g., lot size or house size), the observation cannot be used in the analysis. Therefore, it was necessary to decide which characteristics to include in any of the analyses. For instance, if data on whether a home has central air conditioning were reported on only one-third of the sales transactions, only those transactions with central air conditioning could be used in the analysis and fully two-thirds of the transactions were not usable. To keep missing data cells from limiting the analysis, data fields that were missing a sizable number of observations were not included in the regression analysis.

2. Academic research generally presents the descriptive statistics of the data first and later discusses how these data are used in the quantitative analysis in the form of variable descriptions. But because few of the data fields are transformed, a discussion of variables is presented first and then followed by the summary statistics for each variable. This method seems to be the best way to present the data on multiple communities without being overly redundant.

3. A binary variable is one that has a value of 0 or 1. Binary or "dummy" variables hold the value of 1 if a property maintains a particular attribute and 0 if it does not. For example, if a house has a basement, *BASEMENT* would be assigned a value of 1; if it does not, it would be assigned a value of 0. Because most municipalities and data sources do not provide any quality information on the condition or size of basement space, the best way to represent the existence of a basement in a regression model is with a binary variable (i.e., a house either has a basement or it does not).

4. The "reference variable" is the one variable that other variables are compared to. For instance, when a group of binary variables are used to represent the exteriors of houses, a binary variable *BRICK* might hold a value of 1 if the house has a brick exterior and a 0 otherwise. A value of 0 does not mean, however, that the house has no exterior; it simply means that the house does not have a brick exterior. When defining binary variables, it is necessary to compare each binary variable to properties that do not maintain that characteristic. Therefore, the variable that most frequently shows up in the data, vinyl siding exteriors in this example, is made the reference variable.

5. Data for other communities include sales transactions of single-family detached homes only.

6. The data include both single-family detached houses and townhouses.

7. The township of Chapel Hill, defined by the Orange County Tax Office, includes the entire city of Chapel Hill and its surrounding area.

8. Given the large number of categories of quality (a total of 51), it was inappropriate to use a binary variable to represent each category. For Southern Village, therefore, construction quality was measured using a scalar variable, *GRADE*.

9. To be consistent, townhouses in the Kentlands data set were excluded from the combined data set.

7

How consumers value the attributes of single-family housing

This chapter explains single-family home prices using regression and the data described in Chapter 6. Between 18 and 32 independent variables were used to estimate the actual purchase price (recorded on the deed of sale) of single-family homes. Of particular interest to this study is the effect that a binary variable representing new urbanist communities has on prices of single-family homes. After a discussion of how to interpret regression results, analytical findings are reported for each of the four selected communities—Kentlands, Harbor Town, Laguna West, and Southern Village—and for the combined community data set.

Interpreting the Regression Results

The following discussion is a step-by-step interpretation of a regression model. Based on a subset of the Kentlands data and a subset of the independent variables used to analyze Kentlands, a simplified regression analysis is presented using six independent variables and 100 observations. Step 1 begins with a proposed relationship between the price of a single-family house and a set of housing amenities. Step 2 presents how regression estimates the implicit value of each amenity. Step 3 reveals the results of estimation. And in Step 4, the results of the regression are used to estimate the value of a single-family house.

Step 1. Selecting Housing Attributes
From Chapter 5, we know that the price of a single-family home can be estimated

based on a home's amenities. To accurately estimate the price of a single-family home, it is important to include all factors that are important to homebuyers when purchasing a home. To keep the following example manageable, however, a set of six attributes is used to explain or estimate the purchase price of a single-family house. The first equation in Figure 7-1 states that the price of a single-family home is a function of lot size, living area, number of bathrooms, existence of a basement, number of fireplaces, and physical depreciation. In other words, the price of a home can be explained based on these attributes.

Step 2. Specifying the Model Used To Estimate the Price Of Single-Family Houses
Regression analysis determines the best relationship between the actual sale price

recorded on the deed and the estimated sale price based on the set of housing attributes. Consumer preferences should indicate a relationship between each of the six amenities and house price. For instance, each additional square foot of lot should positively affect the price of a house. To measure this relationship, the coefficient or estimated price per square foot of a lot is multiplied by the lot size to determine the implicit value of the land. The same calculation is then completed for the value of each square foot of living area. After multiplying the coefficient for each of these amenities by the housing amenity, the estimated house price is determined by summing each product.

The estimation model in Step 2 of Figure 7-1 can be described in terms of slope and intercept. The intercept term is the constant. The constant term in a regression model describes the price of a home,

Figure 7-1
Explanation of the Regression Results

Step 1. Selecting Housing Attributes
Price = f (Lot Size, Living Area, Number of Bathrooms, Existence of a Basement, Number of Fireplaces, Physical Depreciation)

Step 2. Specifying the Model Used to Estimate the Price of Single-Family Houses

Estimated Price = Constant
+ Coefficient of *LOT* x Lot Size in Square Feet
+ Coefficient of *AREA* x Square Footage of Living Area
+ Coefficient of *BATH* x Number of Bathrooms
+ Coefficient of *BASEMENT* x Binary Variable of Basement
+ Coefficient of *FIREPLACE* x Number of Fireplaces
+ Coefficient of *AGE* x Age of Property

Step 3. Estimating the Model

Housing Attribute	Variable	Coefficient[†]	t-Statistic
	Constant	20,000	6.53
Lot Size	*LOT*	6.50	7.17
Living Area	*AREA*	62	12.71
Number of Bathrooms	*BATH*	9,500	4.50
Existence of a Basement	*BASEMENT*	10,300	2.24
Number of Fireplaces	*FIREPLACE*	9,490	2.88
Age of Property	*AGE*	−2,883	−8.02
F-Statistic		457.34	
R²		.8639	

[†] Coefficients were estimated using 100 sales transactions in zip code 20878 in 1997.

Step 4. Interpreting the Estimation Results

Variable	Coefficient	Variable Value	Implicit Component Price[††]
Constant	20,000		$20,000
LOT	6.50	8,500	55,250
AREA	62	2,100	130,200
BATH	9,500	2.5	23,750
BASEMENT	10,300	1	10,300
FIREPLACE	9,490	1	9,490
AGE	−2,883	4	−11,532
Estimated House Price			$237,458

[††] Product of coefficient and variable value.

holding all housing attributes *constant* at zero.[1] The slope is formed by the set of amenities times its multiplier or coefficient (referred to in more technical terms as a "parameter estimate"). This equation reveals the price that consumers are willing to pay for a particular set of amenities.

Step 3. Estimating the Model

Figure 7-1 presents the estimation results with the important regression statistics. First, the *F*-statistic is much larger than 4, indicating that the proposed relationship is not attributable to chance at the 99 percent level of certainty. Second, the explanatory power of the model is in the reasonable range of 80 to 95 percent for a single-family regression analysis. With a credible estimation model established, we can now look at the sign (positive or negative) of the relationships between the sale price and each of the independent variables (lot size, living area, number of bathrooms, basement, number of fireplaces, and property age). As expected, the sign of each of the independent variables is positive except for the age coefficient. In other words, an additional square foot of lot or living area, or another bathroom or fireplace, or the existence of a basement has a positive effect on the sale price. Age, on the other hand, has a negative relationship to the sale price of a property. This conclusion also makes sense, because the older a house, the less value it has, holding all else equal.

Next, we assess the strength of the relationship between each of the independent variables and the dependent variable (the sale price of the house). For all coefficients, the *t*-statistic is greater than 2 or less than –2, indicating that each of the independent variables is important to the model at the 95 percent level.

Step 4. Interpreting the Estimation Results

The final step in Figure 7-1 values a typical single-family home in the 20878 zip code (Kentlands). The typical home sits on an 8,500-square-foot lot, has 2,100 square feet

of living space, 2.5 bathrooms, a basement, and a fireplace, and is four years old. Using the price equation in Step 2, we can estimate the price of this home based on these six housing attributes. To estimate the price, we must multiply each attribute or variable by the coefficient for that attribute.

The estimated price of the home is the sum of the products of the lot size times the lot coefficient (8,500 square feet times $6.50 per square foot), the living area times the living area coefficient (2,100 square feet times $62.00 per square foot), the number of bathrooms times the bathroom coefficient (2.5 bathrooms times $9,500 per bathroom), whether a basement exists times the basement coefficient (one basement times $10,300 per basement), the number of fireplaces times the fireplace coefficient (one fireplace times $9,490 per fireplace), the age of the house times the age coefficient (four years old times –$2,883), and the value of the constant ($20,000). Thus, $237,458 is the estimated price of the house.

Figures 7-2 through 7-6 present two regression models. Results of the linear form model are presented in the first two columns. The linear form (constant returns-to-scale) is interpreted in the same way as the previous example; for each unit change in the independent variables (i.e., an additional square foot of lot, an additional bathroom, and so on), the dependent variable changes a set dollar amount. The third and fourth columns depict the semi-log form (i.e., diminishing returns-to-scale). In this form, each unit change in the independent variable creates a percent change in the dependent variable. While a variety of models are estimated, the results of the linear and semi-log functional forms are easiest to interpret. (The other functional forms returned results that were very similar to those presented in these figures.) Although both the linear and semi-log models are presented in each figure, only the linear model is discussed.

Kentlands

Figure 7-2 presents the regression results and the important diagnostic statistics for the Kentlands market area. First, the F-statistic is significant at the 99 percent level, denoting that the proposed relationship is not attributable to chance. Second, the R-squared is 91.5 percent, indicating that more than 90 percent of the variation in single-family home prices is explained with this model specification. Both of these credibility measures of the regression model are in line with prior research and our expectations.

Figure 7-2

Single-Family Home Sale Prices for Kentlands

	Linear Form		Semi-log Form	
	Coefficient	t-Statistic	Coefficient	t-Statistic
INTERCEPT	−145,613	−12.03	10.73	207.42
Site Characteristics				
LOGLOT	26,950	19.13	.12	19.99
PARKING	6,683	4.97	.04	7.93
Interior Characteristics				
AREA (10⁻³)	48,999	31.84	.15	22.89
BATH	13,591	12.62	.06	13.62
BASEMENT	4,535	2.32	.04	4.86
FIREPLACE	9,490	7.97	.04	8.29
Exterior Characteristics				
WSHINGLE	5,363	2.40	.01	1.38
ALUMINUM	1,186	.74	−.02	−2.45
BRICK	16,104	7.13	.01	1.07
STORY1	18,363	6.13	.05	3.60
STORY3	−29,791	−6.91	−.10	−5.63
SPLITFOYER	20,962	4.47	.06	3.13
TOWNHOME	−7,166	−2.89	−.10	−10.34
Quality Characteristics				
GRADE3	−5,671	−1.64	−.09	−6.05
GRADE5	19,388	10.04	.08	10.38
GRADE6	62,364	14.74	.13	7.30
AGE	−2,883	−12.20	−.01	−13.53
AGESQUARE (10⁻³)	25,072	4.76	.12	5.59
Location Characteristics				
C7006.01	−21,341	−7.09	−.05	−4.28
C7006.04	−6,269	−2.24	−.01	−1.10
C7006.05	1,014	.45	.01	1.20
C7006.06	12,768	4.96	.04	3.60
C7006.07	12,763	5.39	.04	4.22
C7007.06	−21,326	−5.09	−.11	−6.46
C7008.01	−8,021	−2.88	−.06	−5.55
C7008.05	−14,030	−5.37	−.05	−4.59
Market Characteristics				
YEAR95	−1,160	−.81	.00	.28
YEAR96	−1,425	−.92	−.00	−.69
YEAR97	−1,213	−.66	.01	.88
KENTLANDS	24,603	7.45	.13	9.59
F-Statistic	847.56		864.88	
R²	.9150		.9166	

The dependent variable is the sale price recorded on the deed.

The next diagnostic is to see whether the model reflects rational consumer behavior. Site and interior characteristics of the properties are where the strongest expectations of consumer behavior occur. As expected, site and interior characteristics are positively related to house price. Of the exterior characteristics, wood-shingled roofs *(WSHINGLE)* and brick exteriors *(BRICK)* both have a positive effect on single-family house prices, as expected. Conversely, townhouses have a negative relationship with price, also as anticipated. No prior expectations existed for the effect that the number of stories should have on the price of a single-family home.

Binary variables for construction quality also maintained the expected relationship with house price. Three binary variables were included *(GRADE3, GRADE5,* and *GRADE6),* with grade 4 the reference variable. Because grade 4 was the reference, the other variables were compared with a house of quality grade 4. As grade 3 is inferior to the reference variable, it was expected that consumers would pay a discount for a grade 3 property, which is what the regression results reveal. Conversely, properties with grades of 5 and 6 are superior to grade 4, and the regression results reveal a premium for these two grades. The expected negative coefficient for age reveals that an older home is worth less than a newer home, and the *AGESQUARE* positive coefficient indicates that the relationship between house value and house age is not linear. No prior expectations existed for the location variables defined by census tracts.

The market characteristics of *YEAR95, YEAR96,* and *YEAR97* (with sales in 1994 as the reference variable) indicate that for zip code 20878, the price of single-family homes has declined slightly since 1994. Of most interest to this study is the *KENTLANDS* binary variable. The positive coefficient of this variable indicates that consumers pay more to live in Kentlands relative to the area surrounding it.

The final diagnostic test is to assess the *t*-statistic for each independent variable.

The *t*-statistic measures the unique explanatory power of each independent variable, holding other independent variables constant. All the *t*-statistics for the variables for which we had prior expectations are significant at the 5 percent level (i.e., have a *t*-statistic of greater than 2 or less than –2), except the *GRADE3* variable. The construction quality grade of 3 is significant at the 10 percent level, however, which means that the difference between grade 3 and grade 4 construction quality is not significantly different from zero 95 percent of the time. The *KENTLANDS* variable maintained a *t*-statistic of 7.45, revealing a strong positive relationship between being located in Kentlands and price of a single-family home, holding other housing attributes constant.

Harbor Town

Figure 7-3 presents the regression results for Harbor Town's market area. First, the *F*-statistic is significant at the 99 percent level, and the *R*-squared is 90.5 percent, indicating a credible model that explains more than 90 percent of the variation in single-family home prices.

All site and interior characteristics are positively related to house price, which reflects our thoughts on how consumers value these attributes. Exterior facade is represented by a series of binary variables, including *FRAME* (wood exterior), *STUCCO* (stucco exterior), *VINYL* (vinyl siding exterior), *STONE* (stone exterior), and *BRICKFRAME* (frame with a brick exterior), with the reference variable being brick exterior. Different from expectations, the stone exterior maintains a negative value or relationship to house price. Only 1 percent of transactions had a stone exterior, however, a number too small to return a credible estimate. No prior expectations existed on the effect that the number of stories and type of roof structure should have on the price of a single-family home.

Binary variables for construction quality also maintained the expected relation-

Figure 7-3

Single-Family Home Sale Prices for Harbor Town

	Linear Form		Semi-log Form	
	Coefficient	t-Statistic	Coefficient	t-Statistic
INTERCEPT	−33,851	−1.85	10.06	64.79
Site Characteristics				
LOGLOT	5,279	2.59	.06	3.98
PARKING	3,782	2.66	.02	2.17
Interior Characteristics				
AREA (10⁻³)	47,420	15.36	.35	13.36
BATH	4,614	1.94	.04	2.04
BASEMENT	762	.30	−.03	−1.67
FIREPLACE	4,358	3.13	.03	3.21
Exterior Characteristics				
FRAME	7,394	2.80	.05	2.39
STUCCO	7,374	1.37	.07	1.63
VINYL	5,330	1.52	.01	.56
STONE	−14,284	−1.93	−.18	−2.98
BRICKFRAME	−17,551	−2.83	−.10	−2.01
HIP	−856	−.33	−.01	−.63
STORY2	−2,086	−.56	.06	2.00
STORY3	6,625	1.01	.03	.71
Quality Characteristics				
GRADE4	−22,803	−2.18	−.68	−7.69
GRADE5	671	.27	−.06	−3.00
GRADE7	21,625	5.22	.28	7.98
GRADE8	41,375	7.76	.33	7.40
GRADE9	88,900	12.56	.46	7.67
GRADE10	114,211	8.86	.33	3.00
AGE	−550	−2.53	−.01	−2.78
AGESQUARE (10⁻³)	1,358	.55	.03	1.66
Location Characteristics				
MUDISLAND	−28,508	−5.81	−.21	−5.24
Market Characteristics				
YEAR95	5,494	2.07	.06	2.88
YEAR96	9,200	3.55	.11	5.44
YEAR97	16,626	6.49	.15	6.96
GATED	66,382	7.29	.44	5.77
HARBORTOWN	30,690	5.24	.25	5.08
F-Statistic	**225.10**		**199.81**	
R^2	**.9046**		**.8938**	

The dependent variable is the sale price recorded on the deed.

ship with house price, with the exception of *GRADE5*. Six binary variables were included *(GRADE4, GRADE5, GRADE7, GRADE8, GRADE9,* and *GRADE10),* with grade 6 the reference variable. Because grade 6 was the reference, the other variables were compared with a house of quality grade 6. As grades 4 and 5 are inferior to the reference variable, it was expected

that consumers would pay less for a home with these lower construction grades. While grade 5 carries a small and insignificant coefficient, it was unexpectedly positive. Grades 7 through 10 are superior to construction quality grade 6, and the regression results reveal a premium. The expected negative coefficient for age reveals that an older home is worth less than a newer home, and the *AGESQUARE* positive coefficient indicates that the relationship between house value and house age is not linear. The single location variable, *MUD-ISLAND*, indicates that housing units on Mud Island sell for less than comparable properties off the island.

The market characteristics indicate that in the Harbor Town market area, single-family home prices have increased in value each year since 1994. Additionally, consumers pay a premium to live in a gated community. Of greatest importance to this study is the *HARBORTOWN* binary variable. The positive value of this variable indicates that consumers pay more to live in Harbor Town compared with the area surrounding it.

All the *t*-statistics for the variables for which we had prior expectations are significant at the 5 percent level except *BASE-MENT* and *GRADE5*. It is difficult to explain why the coefficient for basement is not significant, but one possible explanation is the proximity to the Mississippi River and the possibility of flooding in this market area. The *HARBORTOWN* variable maintained a *t*-statistic of 5.24, revealing a strong positive relationship between being located in Harbor Town and price of a single-family home, holding other housing attributes constant.

Laguna West

Figure 7-4 presents the regression results and the important diagnostic statistics for the Laguna West market area. First, the *F*-statistic is significant at the 99 percent level, denoting a useful model. Second, the *R*-squared is 86.6 percent, indicating that almost 90 percent of the variation in single-family home prices is explained with this model specification.

All site and interior characteristics are positively related to house price, as expected. Of the exterior characteristics, consumers are largely indifferent to whether a roof is wood-shingled or composite-shingled, and exhibit a slight preference for stucco over wood exterior finishes. The *POOL* variable has a positive relationship with the price of a home.

Binary variables for construction quality also maintained the expected relationship with house price. Three binary variables were included *(EXCELLENT, GOOD,* and *POOR),* with average construction quality the reference variable. Because "average" was the reference variable, the other variables were compared with a house of average quality. As poor quality is inferior to the reference variable, it was expected that consumers would pay less for poor quality, which is what the regression results reveal. Conversely, good and excellent quality are higher than average quality, and the regression results show that consumers pay more for these two grades. The expected negative coefficient for age reveals that an older home is worth less than a newer home. Again, no prior expectations existed for the location variable defined by census tract.

The market characteristics indicate that in the Laguna West market area, single-family home prices have declined since 1994. *GATED* and *LAKEVIEW* reveal that both gated communities and properties with lake views sell for a premium. The coefficient of the *LAGUNAWEST* binary variable is also positive. All the *t*-statistics for the variables for which we had prior expectations are significant at the 5 percent level. The *LAGUNAWEST* variable maintained a *t*-statistic of 6.06.

Southern Village

Figure 7-5 presents the regression results and the diagnostic statistics for the Southern Village market area. First, the *F*-statistic is significant at the 99 percent level, denoting that the proposed relationship is not attributable to chance. Second, the *R*-squared is 84.8 percent, indicating that a vast

Figure 7-4
Single-Family Home Sale Prices for Laguna West

	Linear Form		Semi-log Form	
	Coefficient	t-Statistic	Coefficient	t-Statistic
INTERCEPT	−72,078	−10.71	10.37	244.80
Site Characteristics				
LOGLOT	11,897	14.62	.09	18.48
PARKING	4,938	8.27	.02	6.79
Interior Characteristics				
AREA (10^{-3})	58,687	69.37	.37	70.13
BATH	4,069	3.46	.01	.77
Exterior Characteristics				
COMPOSITE	457	.47	−.01	−1.95
WOOD	−1,325	−1.33	−.01	−1.94
POOL	9,163	9.26	.05	7.99
STORY2	−5,962	−6.93	−.01	−2.66
Quality Characteristics				
EXCELLENT	14,260	4.31	.07	3.44
GOOD	10,281	14.95	.05	11.76
POOR	−7,579	−2.67	−.06	−3.60
AGE	−1,030	−9.52	−.01	−10.27
AGESQUARE (10^{-3})	7,177	1.91	−.03	−.1.67
Location Characteristics				
C96.04	1,591	1.92	.00	.37
Market Characteristics				
YEAR95	−4,722	−8.23	−.02	−8.12
YEAR96	−8,490	−15.05	−.05	−15.45
YEAR97	−8,748	−11.83	−.06	−13.09
GATED	28,752	11.22	.12	7.63
LAKEVIEW	22,664	14.34	.14	14.82
LAGUNAWEST	5,157	6.06	.04	7.47
F-Statistic	**1,059.96**		**1,086.16**	
R^2	**.8660**		**.8688**	

The dependent variable is the sale price recorded on the deed.

majority of the variation in single-family home prices is explained with this model specification.

All site and interior characteristics are positively related to house price, except tile flooring, as expected.[2] Interior floor surfaces were grouped into one of three binary categories: carpeting, hardwood, and tile. Of the three, hardwood floors positively affect the price of a home. Of the exterior characteristics, consumers prefer composite-shingled roofs to metal-shingled roofs, and are generally indifferent to hip and gable roof structures. Additionally, this market preferred two-story

houses to single-story houses and masonry basements to poured concrete basements.

Construction quality was a scalar variable and maintained the expected relationship with house price—the higher the quality, the higher the price. The expected negative coefficient for age reveals that an older home is worth less than a newer one.

The Southern Village market area for single-family homes has seen strong property appreciation since 1994. The positive value of *SOUTHERN* indicates that consumers pay more to live in Southern Village than the area surrounding it.

Figure 7-5
Single-Family Home Sale Prices for Southern Village

	Linear Form		Semi-log Form	
	Coefficient	t-Statistic	Coefficient	t-Statistic
INTERCEPT	−4,353	−.18	11.22	100.69
Site Characteristics				
LOT (10^{-3})	276	1.94	.00	1.06
SMALL	18,061	4.45	.08	4.09
PARKING	1,190	.76	.01	1.59
Interior Characteristics				
AREA (10^{-3})	83,034	23.95	.37	22.59
ADDITION (10^{-3})	24,990	1.12	.12	1.12
BATH	38,146	12.49	.15	10.66
BASEMENT	3,601	.90	.02	1.13
FIREPLACE	10,337	2.78	.07	3.94
HARDWOOD	8,147	2.92	.01	1.44
TILE	−1,256	−.14	.00	.22
Exterior Characteristics				
METAL	−16,639	−1.67	−.17	−3.56
HIP	644	.22	−.01	−.76
SLAB	−18,114	−1.82	−.05	−1.25
STORY1	−54,715	−13.39	−.31	−16.03
Quality Characteristics				
GRADE	10,563	1.02	.09	1.83
AGE	−1,326	−3.65	−.01	−3.46
AGESQUARE (10^{-3})	17,441	2.84	.08	2.71
Location Characteristics				
C107.01	−41,514	−2.09	−.22	−2.30
C107.02	−27,499	−1.55	−.14	−1.69
C107.03	−25,125	−1.29	−.11	−1.27
C107.04	−23,432	−1.24	−.14	−1.62
C112.01	−34,207	−1.92	−.16	−1.92
C112.02	−38,372	−2.14	−.18	−2.14
C112.98	−28,603	−1.35	−.12	−1.25
C113	−41,467	−2.25	−.20	−2.31
C117	−15,740	−.90	−.06	−.83
C118	−16,969	−.94	−.10	−1.25
C122	−39,178	−2.24	−.20	−2.39
Market Characteristics				
YEAR95	8,382	2.58	.04	3.11
YEAR96	14,114	4.23	.07	4.51
YEAR97	19,257	4.90	.09	5.21
SOUTHERN	16,334	4.77	.09	5.47
F-Statistic	**81.76**		**87.80**	
R²	**.8477**		**.8567**	

The dependent variable is the sale price recorded on the deed.

Most of the *t*-statistics for the variables for which we had prior expectations are significant at the 5 percent level with the exception of *PARKING, ADDITION,* and *BASEMENT.* Although these three variables maintained the expected sign, they are not significant at the 5 percent level. The abundance of on-street parking available at Southern Village could explain the insignificance of covered parking. *ADDITION* refers to the square feet of additional nonliving space. Because the quality of this space was not measured, the lack of significance for this variable is not of great concern. Although the basement variable was expected to be significant, much like Harbor Town, however, basement space did not appear to be of great importance to consumers. The *SOUTHERN* variable maintained a *t*-statistic of 4.77, revealing a strong positive relationship between location in Southern Village and price of a single-family home, holding other housing attributes constant.

Combined Data Set

Figure 7-6 presents the regression results for the combined data set for the four communities. First, the *F*-statistic is significant at the 99 percent level. Second, the *R*-squared is 90.8 percent, indicating that more than 90 percent of the variation in single-family home prices is explained with this model specification.

All site and interior characteristics were positively related to house price, reflecting consumers' behavior. The only exterior characteristics common across all data sets were those referring to number of stories. Based on these results, consumers pay more for single-story homes than for two- and three-story homes.

Construction quality for each municipality was standardized on a scale of 0 and 1 and included as a scalar variable in the

Figure 7-6
Single-Family Home Sale Prices for Combined Data Set

	Linear Form		Semi-log Form	
	Coefficient	t-Statistic	Coefficient	t-Statistic
INTERCEPT	−202,775	−28.63	10.07	254.46
Site Characteristics				
LOGLOT	15,088	18.41	.09	21.81
PARKING	6,039	9.04	.05	15.02
Interior Characteristics				
AREA (10^{-3})	55,467	60.22	.25	48.50
BATH	16,803	17.23	.06	11.77
BASEMENT	6,678	4.76	.04	5.12
FIREPLACE	4,088	4.36	.05	10.34
Exterior Characteristics				
STORY1	10,244	10.03	−.03	−5.86
STORY3	−10,315	−2.30	.16	6.54
Quality Characteristics				
GRADE	126,021	22.24	.39	12.48
AGE	−1,249	−13.16	−.01	−17.58
AGESQUARE (10^{-3})	10,273	7.80	.06	8.94
Location Characteristics				
MD	74,603	41.68	.36	36.96
TN	6,259	2.96	−.13	−11.44
NC	52,060	22.49	.32	25.23
Market Characteristics				
YEAR95	−2,864	−3.06	−.01	−1.89
YEAR96	−4,980	−5.33	−.01	−2.96
YEAR97	−2,488	−2.38	.00	.51
NU	20,189	17.50	.11	18.03
F-Statistic	**3,196.70**		**3,110.55**	
R²	.9082		.9059	

The dependent variable is the sale price recorded on the deed.

combined analysis. Quality of construction positively affects house price. The expected negative coefficient on age reveals that an older home is worth less than a newer home, and the positive coefficient *AGESQUARE* indicates that the relationship between house value and house age is not linear.

The market characteristics *YEAR95*, *YEAR96*, and *YEAR97* (with sales in 1994 as the reference variable) indicate that for the four markets, single-family home prices declined slightly since 1994. Of greatest importance to this study is the NU binary variable. The positive value of this variable indicates that consumers pay more to live in new urbanist communities than conventional communities in surrounding areas.

All the *t*-statistics for all the variables are significant at the 5 percent level. The new urbanism binary variable maintained a *t*-statistic of 17.50, revealing a strong positive relationship with the price of a single-family home.

The expected economic relationship between the dependent variable (house price) and the independent variables (the housing attributes) was in most all cases as expected and significant. Across all analyses and across functional form (linear and semi-log), the new urbanism binary variable was positive and significant.

Notes

1. For a more complete discussion of the interpretation of the constant term (or intercept), see J.F. Hair, R.E. Anderson, R.L. Tatham, and W.C. Black, *Multivariate Data Analysis,* 4th ed. (Englewood Cliffs, N.J.: Prentice-Hall, 1995), p. 81.

2. In the regression analysis of Southern Village, lot size is represented by the square footage of a lot *(LOT)* and a binary variable for lots smaller than one-sixth acre *(SMALL),* because preliminary regression results indicate that models using *LOT* and *SMALL* fit the data better than *LOGLOT*.

Conclusion

The findings of this study reveal that consumers are willing to pay more to live in communities designed with principles of the new urbanism compared with surrounding conventional developments. In the regression analyses, the binary variable representing the new urbanism is always positive and statistically significant, meaning that homebuyers pay more for houses in new urbanist communities than for properties with comparable housing characteristics in conventional suburban developments.

Each regression model estimates the actual sale price of a home using lot size, house size, interior housing characteristics, exterior housing attributes, quality of construction, location, and market characteristics. In other words, the price of single-family homes was determined using the attributes important to homebuyers, resulting in the ability to explain 85 to 92 percent of the variation in sale prices of single-family homes.

But what effect does a new urbanist development have on single-family home prices? Figure 8-1 presents the premium for new urbanist design for each development and for all four developments combined. These results are culled from Figures 7-2 through 7-6. The linear form (constant returns-to-scale) and the semi-log form (decreasing returns-to-scale) regression models indicate that consumers are willing to pay more to live in new urbanist communities than in surrounding areas; these results are significant at the 99 percent level across

all models for all communities. The estimated premium ranges from approximately $5,000 for Laguna West to approximately $30,000 for Harbor Town. The combined data set reveals a $20,000 premium for properties in new urbanist communities compared with surrounding neighborhoods. The results of the semi-log form are presented as percents. Properties located in new urbanist

---

Figure 8-1

Estimated New Urbanist Premiums by Community and for All Communities Combined

	Dollar Value*	Percent of Home Value*
Kentlands	$24,603	13
Harbor Town	30,690	25
Laguna West	5,157	4
Southern Village	16,334	9
Combined	20,189	11

* All estimated premiums are significant at the 1 percent level.

developments command a premium of 4 to 25 percent over surrounding communities, with the combined data set showing an 11 percent premium.

Critics of the new urbanism have suggested that any premium resulting from urbanist development reflects a higher quality of construction in new urbanist communities. This analysis, however, explicitly accounts for property-by-property differences in construction quality, property age, and interior and exterior housing attributes, and finds that a price premium for new urbanist development still exists. Although no model can perfectly separate these effects from the community and planning characteristics in new urbanist developments, the size and consistency of the premium for the new urbanism across all communities suggest that consumers find new urbanist projects desirable and are willing to pay more to reside in them.

While it is clear that consumers are willing to pay more to live in new urbanist communities, which attributes of new urbanist communities are important to consumers is a question that remains for future research. Is it the interconnected streets, the sidewalks, or treeboxes that charm consumers? Or the short setbacks and front porches? Or the placement of garages in the rear and the architectural continuity? Or the mix of residential and nonresidential land uses? Or the synergy of all these factors combined?

The premium for the new urbanism does not indicate, however, that developers make more money with new urbanist developments. Little information is available on the cost to develop new urbanist communities, and it is therefore not possible to comment on the profitability of these developments. This subject is clearly worthy of study.

And it is not possible to comment on whether the premium for the new urbanism reflects the behavior of all or even a majority of consumers. Currently, the number of new urbanist units is a small portion of total residential development in each market area studied. Whether new urbanist communities have mass appeal remains untested. It is quite clear, however, that a portion of homebuyers find the set of amenities provided by new urbanist developments more desirable than the amenities provided in conventional development.

The enthusiasm displayed by developers, planners, municipal officials, environmentalists, and residents for this comparative study is encouraging. It provides some commentary on the future interest in—possibly even the future viability of—new types of residential development.

The hedonic price model

This study uses the hedonic price model to assess the effects of the new urbanism on the value of single-family residences. Hedonic analysis has been used extensively in housing market research in estimating the demand for housing and neighborhood attributes,[1] constructing constant-quality housing price indices,[2] analyzing the impact of neighborhood externalities on house prices,[3] and estimating the benefits of public investment programs.[4] This appendix reviews the literature on the hedonic price model and discusses both the theoretical framework of the model and the empirical issues that researchers have found in specifying the hedonic function.

Theoretical Foundations of the Hedonic Price Model

The hedonic price model[5] describes the relationship between the observed prices of goods and the characteristics associated with the commodities, based on the hypothesis that "goods are valued for their utility-bearing attributes or characteristics."[6] Rosen defines hedonic prices as the prices of attributes that can be disclosed by economic agents from the market prices of products and the amounts of characteristics contained in the products.

Consider the market for a class of commodities that are differentiated by n objectively measured characteristics. Each product has a market price, p, and offers consumers a distinct package of attributes that is completely described by the vector $z = (z_1, z_2, ..., z_n)$, with z_i measuring the amount of the ith characteristic contained in each product. The hedonic price model assumes that a wide variety of alternative packages of attributes are available and that the market is competitive as individual agents are price takers. Both consumers and producers in the market are utility maximizers. In equilibrium, there exists a hedonic function, f, that links the price of each product with its characteristics, i.e., $p(z) = f(z_1, z_2, ..., z_n)$. The hedonic function is determined by the market-clearing condition that the amount of each commodity offered by sellers must be equal to the amount demanded by consumers.[7]

The estimated hedonic price-characteristic relationships typically identify neither the consumer's demand function nor the producer's supply function. Instead, the hedonic price function reflects only the set of market-clearing prices associated with the utility-bearing attributes. Only if consumers are identical while suppliers differ will the hedonic price function trace out the demand function for the specific product. Similarly, if all suppliers are identical but consumers differ, the hedonic function identifies the supply curve.[8]

Application to the Housing Market

Housing can be defined as a heterogeneous commodity differentiated into a bundle of attributes. The hedonic price function establishes a functional relationship between the market-clearing housing price, *P(H)*, and the level of attributes contained in the housing unit:

$$P(H) = f(h_1, h_2, ..., h_k),$$

where $H = (h_1, h_2, ..., h_k)$ is the vector of attributes. This vector of housing attributes may include structural traits of the property (e.g., square footage of living area, number of bathrooms, and number of fireplaces); amenities (e.g., availability of a swimming pool); and neighborhood characteristics (e.g., air quality, school district, and traffic conditions).

The prices of individual housing features are not directly observable, because no explicit markets exist for those features. Instead, the transactions of housing traits are carried out through implicit markets that make up the housing market. The price of any attribute *k* contained in *H*, $P_k (\equiv \partial \Pi(H)/ \partial h_k)$, is referred to as the equilibrium marginal price of the attribute. With knowledge of the property price and the composition of housing traits and a proper specification of the functional relationship, the marginal attribute price is revealed by estimating the parameters of the hedonic price function. Notice that no information about the individual characteristics of the consumers or the suppliers is necessary.

Empirical Issues in the Specification of the Hedonic Function

Economic theory has developed a robust set of properties about the demand and supply curves of the housing market but places very few restrictions on the form of the hedonic price function. Because the theory provides little guidance concerning the choice of the proper functional form, the selection of the exact set of housing attributes, and the precise definition of the housing market, implementation of the hedonic price model is not an easy task.[9] These empirical issues have drawn considerable attention in the literature as researchers strive to develop the ideal specification. The following sections discuss three sources of empirical problems that appear in the literature.

Functional Form of the Hedonic Price Model

The empirical issue that has received the most attention is choosing the proper functional form of the hedonic price function. Early studies using the hedonic price model chose the basic functional forms, such as linear, semi-log, and log-log, for their simplicity. As researchers[10] realized that an incorrect functional form may induce inconsistent parameter estimates, however, they started to search for the most appropriate form. Unfortunately, theory offers no guideline to the functional form specification. Rosen suggests using a goodness-of-fit criterion in the selection of functional form,[11] and early studies investigating functional forms follow this approach.[12] The researchers use a likelihood ratio test to compare the more restricted forms with the more complicated forms derived from the Box-Cox transformation.[13] These studies favor the Box-Cox forms, as the transformation process often creates a better fit for the data. Moreover:

The flexible Box-Cox transformation provides a reliable method of identifying amenity relationships without unwar-

ranted restrictions on functional form. In addition, the estimated maximum likelihood Box-Cox results can be used to test the statistical validity of alternative hypotheses about functional form.[14]

Other studies, however, reveal the shortcomings of using the Box-Cox flexible form. "The formal hypothesis testing advantage of the Box-Cox functional form is purchased at the expense of other important goals."[15] For example, the large number of parameters that need to be estimated in the Box-Cox transformation reduces the accuracy of any single coefficient. As a result, the best fit criterion resulting from the likelihood ratio test does not necessarily lead to more precise estimates of implicit marginal prices of housing attributes.[16]

Another limitation of the transformation is that it is not applicable to binary, or dummy, variables. "A major difficulty with applying this Box-Cox functional form search is that 25 of our 30 independent variables are dichotomous (i.e., one if yes, zero otherwise). This is problematic in that the power transformation for these, which include all of our neighborhood traits, must necessarily be linear."[17]

Using the Box-Cox transformation also causes problems of interpretation. For example, "the main disadvantage [of the transformation] is that coefficient interpretation is more difficult."[18] In a linear form hedonic price function, an estimated coefficient is defined as the value added by one more unit of the associated housing attribute; in a semi-log form, a parameter estimate is interpreted as the percentage change in housing value. Unlike the simpler functional forms, interpretation of the parameters estimated with the Box-Cox form is very difficult, and the implicit prices are not revealed directly.

The appropriateness of using the goodness-of-fit criterion in selecting the best functional form has been questioned if the research goal is to value the housing attributes.[19] Thus, the best form for the hedonic price function is the one that produces the smallest errors in estimating the marginal implicit price.[20] Because the computation of estimation errors requires the knowledge of true implicit prices, the comparison can be made only in the context of simulation. An examination of six forms of the hedonic price function found that when all attributes are correctly observed, the linear and quadratic Box-Cox transformations result in the most accurate estimates.[21] When some attributes are not observed or are replaced by proxies, however, the linear Box-Cox form and the simple linear form outperform all others.

From the inconclusive empirical evidence, no single functional form completely dominates others. In consideration of the problems in applying Box-Cox transformations to all variables, a series of models have been estimated with transformations of the dependent variable only. The results of both the semi-log form and the linear form, two special cases with transformation factors equal to 0 and 1, respectively, are presented in this study. Other functional forms were also estimated to test robustness of the model.

Selection of Variables

Another empirical issue is choosing and defining the list of variables for inclusion in the hedonic equation. Ideally, all housing traits considered in valuing a property should be included in the analysis, but some of the attributes cannot easily be defined or observed. In this regard, the literature covers a wide variety of housing characteristics. Some studies give primary importance to structural traits, such as the number of rooms or number of bathrooms, availability of basement, and garage size,[22] some focus on amenities, including negative amenities such as air pollution and aircraft noise, and positive amenities, such as view,[23] some use the assessed value of a property as the sole independent variable,[24] and others emphasize the role of publicly provided neighborhood traits, such as quality schools and public roadways.[25]

Other studies are concerned about the collinearity between housing attributes and thus omit a large number of housing traits.[26] Although the standard errors for the coefficients estimated in the presence of collinearity are biased, removing some of the highly correlated independent variables does not necessarily solve the problem. In fact:

> . . . the omission of variables that should be in the model only confounds the problem because the least squares regressor yields consistent and efficient estimates only when the model is correctly specified. The omission of important traits on the basis of multicollinearity insures that both the standard errors and hedonic coefficients of the remaining traits are biased.[27]

Researchers using the hedonic pricing technique thus face a tradeoff: including highly correlated variables causes collinearity and thus reduces the precision of parameter estimates, while omission of variables that should be in the regression model may result in biased estimates. This study follows the housing valuation literature in selecting the set of independent variables and tests for the possibility of collinearity.

Definition of Housing Submarkets
A third empirical issue that has not drawn as much attention in the literature is the definition of housing markets, or the segmentation of submarkets. Because the hedonic price function represents market-clearing prices, it is important that the sample used to estimate the function be representative of the housing market. Selecting an appropriately defined market can be a problem.

To use too broad a geographical definition of a housing market would produce biased estimates from an improperly aggregated sample. To use too narrow a definition would produce imprecise estimates, because the estimates would not be based on all available information.[28]

Previous studies do not reach a consensus on this empirical issue. Some suggest the use of narrowly defined geographic areas because homebuyers normally are interested in a small geographic area and are insufficiently mobile to take full advantage of any opportunities for arbitrage.[29] Others, however, believe residential migration and housing capital funds are sufficiently mobile across geographic areas to create an efficient housing market.[30]

A systematic study to examine the market homogeneity and/or heterogeneity across areas that estimates hedonic functions with various submarket breakdowns and compares the resultant implicit prices concludes that "there are significant submarket differences in hedonic prices of housing attributes, implying that great care should be taken in the specification of the geographic units for which hedonic models are estimated."[31]

Each hedonic price function in this study is estimated with data drawn from the same zip code, the same neighborhood, or the same township as the new urbanist development under examination; in addition, it uses census tract variables to control for heterogeneity within the zip code.[32] As a result, potential bias that is caused by submarket aggregation should be substantially reduced. In the analysis using a data set that combines all the individual community data sets into one combined data set, the assumption is that a homogeneous market exists across the entire country, at least a homogeneous market for the features offered by the new urbanism.

The literature on the hedonic price model is both deep and broad. Although both the theoretical and empirical issues are well developed in the literature, there is little agreement currently on the best functional specification, number and types of variables, and market definition when estimating a hedonic model. Because of the conflicting literature, a variety of functional forms and model specifications are estimated in this report.

Notes

1. See Nelson (1978), Harrison and Rubinfeld (1978), Blomquist and Worley (1981), Butler (1982), Follain and Jimenez (1985), Do and Sirmans (1994), Rodriguez and Sirmans (1994), and Benson, Hansen, Schwartz, and Smersh (1998).

2. See Goodman (1978), Mark and Goldberg (1984a), Blackley and Follain (1986), Thibodeau (1989), Kiel and Zabel (1997), and Clapp and Giaccotto (1998).

3. See Gabriel and Wolch (1984), Mark and Goldberg (1984b), Grieson and White (1989), Michaels and Smith (1990), Carroll, Clauretie, Jensen, and Waddoups (1996), and Beron, Murdoch, Thayer, and Vijverberg (1997).

4. See Quigley (1982) and Shefer (1990).

5. The development of the hedonic price model has built on the work of Court (1941), Lancaster (1966), and Griliches (1971); however, Rosen's seminal paper (1974) is the most influential contribution to this area.

6. S. Rosen, "Hedonic Prices and Implicit Markets: Product Differentiation in Pure Competition," *Journal of Political Economy,* vol. 82 (1974), p. 34.

7. Ibid., pp. 34–55.

8. P. Linneman, "Hedonic Prices and Residential Location," in *The Economics of Urban Amenities,* ed. D. Diamond and G. Tolley (Orlando: Academic Press, 1982).

9. J.R. Follain and S. Malpezzi, *Dissecting Housing Value and Rent: Estimates of Hedonic Indexes for Thirty-nine Large SMSAs* (Washington, D.C.: The Urban Institute, 1980).

10. See Goodman (1978), Harrison and Rubinfeld (1978), and Blomquist and Worley (1981).

11. Rosen, "Hedonic Prices and Implicit Markets."

12. See Halvorsen and Pollakowski (1981) and Milon, Gressel, and Mulkey (1984).

13. G.E. Box and D.R. Cox, "An analysis of Transformation," *Journal of the Royal Statistical Society,* vol. 26 (1964), pp. 211–52. Box and Cox developed a model that determines the functional specification providing the best fit in terms of log likelihood. The model requires transformation on variable x_i in the following forms and finds the λ that maximizes the log likelihood of the model:

$$\begin{cases} \dfrac{x_i^{\lambda} - 1}{\lambda} & if \ \lambda \neq 0 \\ ln \ x_i & if \ \lambda = 0. \end{cases}$$

14. Milon, Gressel, and Mulkey, "Hedonic Amenity Valuation," p. 386.

15. E. Cassel and R. Mendelsohn, "The Choice of Functional Forms for Hedonic Price Equations: Comment," *Journal of Urban Economics,* vol. 18 (1985), p. 135.

16. Ibid., pp. 135–42.

17. P. Linneman, "Some Empirical Results on the Nature of the Hedonic Price Function for the Urban Housing Market," *Journal of Urban Economics,* vol. 8 (1980b), p. 52.

18. Milon, Gressel, and Mulkey, "Hedonic Amenity Valuation," p. 383.

19. M.L. Cropper, L.B. Deck, and K.E. McConnell, "On the Choice of Functional Form for Hedonic Price Functions," *Review of Economics and Statistics,* vol. 70 (1988), pp. 668–75.

20. Ibid.

21. Ibid. The forms used are linear, semi-log, double-log, quadratic, and Box-Cox transformations of both linear and quadratic variables.

22. See Kain and Quigley (1975), King (1975), Linneman (1980b, 1981), Quigley (1976), Straszheim (1973, 1974, 1975), Case, Pollakowski, and Wachter (1991), Gatzlaff and Ling (1994), Case and Szymanoski (1995), and Meese and Wallace (1997).

23. See Blomquist and Worley (1981), Diamond (1980), Freeman (1979), Harrison and Rubinfeld (1978), Mieszkowski and Saper (1978), Nelson (1978), Do and Sirmans (1994), Rodriguez and Sirmans (1994), and Benson, Hansen, Schwartz, and Smersh (1998).

24. See Clapp, Giaccotto, and Tirtiroglu (1991), and Clapp and Giaccotto (1998).

25. See Edel and Sclar (1974), Linneman (1980a), Oates (1969), Rosen and Fullerton (1977), and Beron, Murdoch, Thayer, and Vijverberg (1997).

26. See, e.g., Linneman, "Hedonic Prices and Residential Location."

27. Ibid., p. 73.

28. Follain and Malpezzi, *Dissecting Housing Value and Rent,* p. 29.

29. See, e.g., Straszheim (1975) and Schaffer (1979).

30. See Butler (1978) and Linneman (1980b).

31. K. Chung, "Hedonic Models of Housing Prices: A Critical Appraisal of the Assumptions," Ph.D. dissertation, Univ. of Texas at Dallas, 1994, p. 84.

32. Census tracts are small, relatively permanent divisions of large cities and adjacent areas whose purpose is to show comparable statistics for small areas. They are relatively homogeneous in characteristics of the population, economic status, and living conditions; the average population is 4,000.

References

Adler, J. "Bye-Bye Suburban Dream." *Newsweek* (May 15, 1995): 40–45.

Altman, L. "Suburban Meets Urban." *Builder* (March 1995): 104, 106.

Appraisal Institute. *The Appraisal of Real Estate.* 11th ed. Chicago: Author, 1996.

Bank of America et al. *Beyond Sprawl: New Patterns of Growth to Fit the New California.* San Francisco: Author, 1995.

Benson, E., J. Hansen, A. Schwartz, Jr., and G. Smersh. "Pricing Residential Amenities: The Value of a View." *Journal of Real Estate Finance and Economics* 16:1 (1998): 55–73.

Beron, K.J., J.C. Murdoch, M.A. Thayer, and W. Vijverberg. "An Analysis of the Housing Market before and after the 1989 Loma Prieta Earthquake." *Land Economics* 73:1 (1997): 101–13.

Binkley, C. "Developers Discover Old Values Can Bring Astonishing Returns." *The Wall Street Journal* (December 4, 1996).

Blackley, D.M., and J.R. Follain. "An Evaluation of Hedonic Price Indexes for Thirty-four Large SMSAs." *Journal of the American Real Estate and Urban Economics Association* 14 (1986): 179–205.

Blomquist, G., and L. Worley. "Hedonic Prices, Demands for Urban Housing Amenities, and Benefit Estimates." *Journal of Urban Economics* 9 (1981): 212–21.

Bookout, L.W. "Neotraditional Town Planning: A New Vision for the Suburbs?" *Urban Land* (January 1992a): 20–26.

———. "Neotraditional Town Planning: Cars, Pedestrians, and Transit." *Urban Land* (February 1992b): 10–15.

Box, G.E., and D.R. Cox. "An Analysis of Transformation." *Journal of the Royal Statistical Society* 26 (1964): 211–52.

Boxer, S. "A Remedy for the Rootlessness of Modern Suburban Life?" *The New York Times* (August 1, 1998).

Bressi, T. "Planning the American Dream." In *The New Urbanism: Toward an Architecture of Community.* Ed. Peter Katz. New York: McGraw-Hill, 1994.

Butler, R. "Hedonic Indexes of Urban Housing: Theory and Problems of Cross-Sectional Estimation." Ph.D. dissertation, Massachusetts Institute of Technology, 1978.

———. "The Specification of Hedonic Indexes for Urban Housing." *Land Economics* 58 (1982): 96–108.

Calthorpe, P. *The Pedestrian Pocketbook.* New York: Princeton Architectural Press, 1989.

———. *The Next American Metropolis: Ecology, Community, and the American Dream.* New York: Princeton Architectural Press, 1993.

Carrns, A. "Architects Attack Development Style." *The Wall Street Journal* (June 11, 1997).

Carroll, T.M., T.M. Clauretie, J. Jensen, and M. Waddoups. "The Economic Impact of a Transient Hazard on Property Value: The 1988 PEPCON Explosion in Henderson, Nevada." *Journal of Real Estate Finance and Economics* 13:2 (1996): 143–67.

Case, B., H.O. Pollakowski, and S.M. Wachter. "On Choosing among House Price Index Methodologies." *Journal of the American Real Estate and Urban Economics Association* 19:3 (1991): 286–307.

Case, B., and E.J. Szymanoski. "Precision in House Price Indices: Findings of a Comparative Study of House Price Index Methods." *Journal of Housing Research* 6:3 (1995): 483–96.

Cassel, E., and R. Mendelsohn. "The Choice of Functional Forms for Hedonic Price Equations: Comment." *Journal of Urban Economics* 18 (1985): 135–42.

Christoforidis, A. "New Alternatives to the Suburb: Neotraditional Developments." *Journal of Planning Literature* 8:4 (May 1994): 429–40.

Chung, K. "Hedonic Models of Housing Prices: A Critical Appraisal of the Assumptions." Ph.D. dissertation, Univ. of Texas at Dallas, 1994.

Clapp, J.M., and C. Giaccotto. "Price Indices Based on the Hedonic Repeat-Sales Method: Application to the Housing Market." *Journal of Real Estate Finance and Economics* 16:1 (1998): 5–26.

Clapp, J.M., C. Giaccotto, and D. Tirtiroglu. "Housing Price Indices: Based on All Transactions Compared to Repeat Subsamples." *Journal of the American Real Estate and Urban Economics Association* 19:3 (1991): 270–85.

Congress for the New Urbanism. "Charter of the New Urbanism." CNU IV, May 3–5, 1996, Charleston, South Carolina.

Constantine, J. "Market Research: Survey of Homebuyers Shows Interest in Traditional Neighborhood Development." *Land Development* (Winter 1994): 5–7.

Consumer Reports. "Neighborhood Reborn." (May 1996): 24–29.

Court, L.M. "Entrepreneurial and Consumer Demand Theories for Commodity Spectra." *Econometrica* 9 (1941): 135–62.

Crane, R. "Cars and Drivers in the New Suburbs: Linking Access to Travel in Neotraditional Planning." *Journal of the American Planning Association* 62:1 (1996): 51–65.

Cropper, M.L., L.B. Deck, and K.E. McConnell. "On the Choice of Functional Form for Hedonic Price Functions." *Review of Economics and Statistics* 70 (1988): 668–75.

Damer, R. "New Urbanism Lives." *Los Angeles Times* (August 9, 1998).

Diamond, D. "The Relationship between Amenities and Urban Land Values." *Land Economics* 51 (1980): 21–32.

Do, A.Q., and C.F. Sirmans. "Residential Property Tax Capitalization: Discount Rate Evidence from California." *National Tax Journal* 47 (1994): 341–48.

Dombrow, J., J.R. Knight, and C.F. Sirmans. "Aggregation Bias in Repeat-Sales Indices." *Journal of Real Estate Finance and Economics* 14:1 (1997): 75–88.

Downs, A. *The Costs of Sprawl: Alternative Forms of Growth.* Transportation Research Conference, May 19, 1998, Minneapolis, Minnesota.

Duany, A., and E. Plater-Zyberk. *Towns and Town-Making Principles.* Cambridge, Mass.: Harvard Univ. Graduate School of Design, 1991.

———. "The Neighborhood, the District, and the Corridor." In *The New Urbanism: Toward an Architecture of Community.* Ed. Peter Katz. New York: McGraw-Hill, 1994.

Edel, M., and T. Sclar. "Taxes, Spending, and Property Values: Supply Adjustments in a Tiebout-Oates World." *Journal of Political Economy* 82 (1974): 941–54.

Ewing, R. "Is Los Angeles–Style Sprawl Desirable?" *Journal of the American Planning Association* 63:1 (1997): 107–26.

Fannie Mae. *1997 National Housing Survey.* Washington, D.C.: Author, 1997.

Flint, A. "Making a Case for Recycling Cities." *The Boston Globe* (February 2, 1998).

Follain, J.R., and E. Jimenez. "Estimating the Demand for Housing Characteristics." *Regional Science and Urban Economics* 15 (1985): 77–107.

Follain, J.R., and S. Malpezzi. *Dissecting Housing Value and Rent: Estimates of Hedonic Indexes for Thirty-nine Large SMSAs.* Washington, D.C.: The Urban Institute, 1980.

Freeman, A. "The Hedonic Price Approach to Measuring Demand for Neighborhood Characteristics." *The Economics of Neighborhood.* Ed. D. Segal. New York: Academic Press, 1979.

Fulton, W. *The New Urbanism: Hope or Hype for American Communities?* Cambridge, Mass.: Lincoln Institute of Land Policy, 1996.

Gabriel, S.A., and J.R. Wolch. "Spillover Effects of Human Service Facilities in a Racially Segmented Housing Market." *Journal of Urban Economics* 16 (1984): 339–50.

Gatzlaff, D.H., and D.C. Ling. "Measuring Changes in Local House Prices: An Empirical Investigation of Alternative Methodologies." *Journal of Urban Economics* 35 (1994): 221–44.

Gelfeld, E. "The Power of Porches." *The Washington Post* (October 8, 1998).

Goldberger, P. "Land of Make Believe." *New Urban News* (September/October 1998): 21.

Goodman, A.C. "Hedonic Prices, Price Indices, and Housing Markets." *Journal of Urban Economics* 5 (1978): 471–84.

Gordon, P., and H.W. Richardson. "Are Compact Cities a Desirable Planning Goal?" *Journal of the American Planning Association* 63:1 (1997): 95–106.

Greene, W. *Econometric Analysis.* 3d ed. Upper Saddle River, N.J.: Prentice-Hall, 1997.

Grieson, R.E., and J.R. White. "The Existence and Capitalization of Neighborhood Externalities: A Reassessment." *Journal of Urban Economics* 25 (1989): 68–76.

Griliches, Zvi, ed. *Price Indexes and Quality Change.* Cambridge, Mass.: Harvard Univ. Press, 1971.

Hair, J.F., R.E. Anderson, R.L. Tatham, and W.C. Black. *Multivariate Data Analysis.* 4th ed. Englewood Cliffs, N.J.: Prentice-Hall, 1995.

Halvorsen, R., and H.O. Pollakowski. "Choice of Functional Form for Hedonic Price Equations." *Journal of Urban Economics* 10 (1981): 34–47.

Harrison, D., and D. Rubinfeld. "Hedonic Housing Prices and the Demand for Clean Air." *Journal of Environmental Economics and Management* 5 (1978): 81–102.

Henderson, R., and A.T. Moore. "Plan Obsolescence." *Reason* (June 1998): 42–47.

Judge, G., R. Hill, W. Griffiths, H. Lutkepohl, and T. Lee. *Introduction to the Theory and Practice of Econometrics.* 2d ed. New York: John Wiley & Sons, 1988.

Kain, J., and J. Quigley. *Housing Markets and Racial Discrimination.* New York: National Bureau of Economic Research, 1975.

Katz, P., ed. *The New Urbanism: Toward an Architecture of Community.* New York: McGraw-Hill, 1994.

Kiel, K.A., and J.E. Zabel. "Evaluating the Usefulness of the American Housing Survey for Creating House Price Indices." *Journal of Real Estate Finance and Economics* 14 (1997): 189–202.

King, A. "The Demand for Housing: Integrating the Roles of Journey-to-Work, Neighborhood Quality, and Prices." *Household Production and Consumption.* Ed. N. Terleckyj. New York: National Bureau of Economic Research, 1975.

Krieger, A. "Whose Urbanism?" *Architecture* (November 1998): 73–77.

Kroloff, R. "Suspending Disbelief." *Architecture* (August 1998): 11.

Kunstler, J.H. *The Geography of Nowhere: The Rise and Decline of America's Man-Made Landscape.* New York: Simon & Schuster, 1994.

———. *Home from Nowhere: Remaking Our Everyday World for the Twenty-first Century.* New York: Simon & Schuster, 1996.

Lancaster, K.J. "A New Approach to Consumer Theory." *Journal of Political Economy* 74 (1966): 132–57.

Landecker, H. "Is New Urbanism Good for America?" *Architecture* (April 1996): 68–77.

Langdon, P. *A Better Place to Live.* Amherst, Mass.: Univ. of Massachusetts Press, 1994.

Linneman, P. "An Empirical Methodology for Analyzing the Properties of Public Goods." *Economic Inquiry* 18 (1980a): 600–617.

———. "Some Empirical Results on the Nature of the Hedonic Price Function for the Urban Housing Market." *Journal of Urban Economics* 8 (1980b): 47–68.

———. "The Demand for Residence Site Characteristics." *Journal of Urban Economics* 9 (1981): 129–48.

———. "Hedonic Prices and Residential Location." *The Economics of Urban Amenities.* Ed. D. Diamond and G. Tolley. Orlando: Academic Press, 1982.

McCosh, J., and L. Soto. "Old-Style New Town Coming." *The Atlanta Journal and Constitution* (July 3, 1998).

Mark, J.H., and M.A. Goldberg. "Alternative Housing Price Indices: An Evaluation." *Journal of the American Real Estate and Urban Economics Association* 12 (1984a): 30–49.

———. "A Study of the Impacts of Zoning on Housing Values over Time." *Journal of Urban Economics* 20 (1984b): 257–73.

Market Perspectives. *Home Buyer Survey: Neotraditional Communities—Kentlands, Harbor Town, Seaside, and Laguna West.* Carmichael, Calif.: Author, 1993.

Marshall, A. "Suburb in Disguise." *Metropolis* 16:1 (July 1996): 70–71+.

Maryland State Department of Assessment and Taxation. *Maryland Assessment CAMA System Manual.* Baltimore: Author, 1996.

Meese, R.A., and N.E. Wallace. "The Construction of Residential Housing Price Indices: A Comparison of Repeat-Sales, Hedonic-Regression, and Hybrid Approaches." *Journal of Real Estate Finance and Economics* 14:1 (1997): 51–74.

Michaels, R.G., and V.K. Smith. "Market Segmentation and Valuing Amenities with Hedonic Models: The Case of Hazardous Waste Sites." *Journal of Urban Economics* 28 (1990): 223–42.

Mieszkowski, P., and A. Saper. "An Estimate of the Effects of Airport Noise on Property Values." *Journal of Urban Economics* 5 (1978): 425–40.

Miles, M.E. "Real Estate as an Asset Class." *Salomon Brothers Research Report* (January 1989).

Miller, P., and J. Moffet. *The Price of Mobility: Uncovering the Hidden Costs of Transportation.* New York: Natural Resources Defense Council, 1993.

Milon, J.W., J. Gressel, and D. Mulkey. "Hedonic Amenity Valuation and Functional Form Specification." *Land Economics* 60 (1984): 378–87.

Mulvihill, D.A. "Inquiry: Is Neotraditional Town Planning a Good Alternative?" *Urban Land* (November 1994): 56.

Muschamp, H. "Can New Urbanism Find Room for the Old?" *The New York Times* (June 2, 1996).

Nelson, J.P. "Residential Choice, Hedonic Prices, and the Demand for Urban Air Quality." *Journal of Urban Economics* 5 (1978): 357–69.

Oates, W. "The Effect of Property Taxes and Local Spending on Property Values: An Empirical Study of Tax Capitalization and the Tiebout Hypothesis." *Journal of Political Economy* 77 (1969): 957–71.

Peek, J., and J.A. Wilcox. "The Measurement and Determinants of Single-Family House Prices." *Journal of the American Real Estate and Urban Economics Association* 19:3 (1991): 353–82.

Quigley, J.M. "Housing Demand in the Short Run: An Analysis of Polytomous Choice." *Explorations in Economic Research* 3 (1976): 76–102.

———. "Nonlinear Budget Constraints and Consumer Demand: An Application to Public Programs for Residential Housing." *Journal of Urban Economics* 12 (1982): 177–201.

Real Estate Research Corporation. *The Costs of Sprawl: Detailed Cost Analysis*. Washington, D.C.: U.S. Government Printing Office, 1974.

Rodriguez, M., and C.F. Sirmans. "Quantifying the Value of a View in Single-Family Housing Markets." *Appraisal Journal* 62 (1994): 600–603.

Rosen, H., and D. Fullerton. "A Note on Local Tax Rates, Public Benefit Levels, and Property Values." *Journal of Political Economy* 85 (1977): 433–40.

Rosen, S. "Hedonic Prices and Implicit Markets: Product Differentiation in Pure Competition." *Journal of Political Economy* 82 (1974): 34–55.

Schaffer, R. "Racial Discrimination in the Boston Housing Market." *Journal of Urban Economics* 6 (1979): 176–96.

Schleimer, J. "Case Study: Are Neo-Traditional Communities Succeeding in the Marketplace?" *Lusk Review* (Fall 1995): 76–82.

Shefer, D. "Estimating Household's Welfare Change with Hedonic Price Method." In *Location and Labor Considerations for Regional Development*. Ed. F. Dietz, W. Heijman, and D. Shefer. Aldershot; Brookfield, USA: Avebury, 1990.

Sherlock, B. "Old-Fashioned Remedy." *Chicago Tribune* (October 4, 1998).

Shields, T. "Urban—With a New Attitude." *The Washington Post* (June 7, 1998).

Singer, P. "New Housing Based on a Colonial Tradition." *The New York Times* (October 25, 1998).

Southworth, M. "Walkable Suburbs? An Evaluation of Neotraditional Communities at the Urban Edge." *Journal of the American Planning Association* 63:1 (1997): 28–44.

Steuteville, R. "Year of Growth for New Urbanism." *New Urban News* (September/October 1998): 1, 3–7.

Straszheim, M. "Estimation of the Demand for Urban Housing Services from Household Interview Data." *The Review of Economics and Statistics* 55 (1973): 1–8.

———. "Hedonic Estimation of Housing Market Prices: A Further Comment." *The Review of Economics and Statistics* 56 (1974): 404–6.

———. *An Econometric Analysis of the Urban Housing Market*. New York: National Bureau of Economic Research, 1975.

Thibodeau, T.G. "Housing Price Indexes from the 1974–1983 SMSA Annual Housing Surveys." *Journal of the American Real Estate and Urban Economics Association* 17 (1989): 100–117.

"Traditional Neighborhood Development Projects in the U.S." *New Urban News* (September/October 1997): 10–13.

U.S. Bureau of the Census. *Census Use Study: Health Information System*. New Haven, Conn.: Author, 1971.

———. *1995 American Housing Survey Data Chart*. Washington, D.C.: Author, 1995.

Wilson, C. "A Town Too Good to Be 'Tru' Like Something Out of a Movie." *USA Today* (June 15, 1998).